MW00654240

GREAT BIG SMALL THINGS

Dale McGlothlin

GREAT BIG
SMALL THINGS

The Extraordinary Life of Fred Selfe:
9 Powerful Lessons of a
Legendary Small College Coach
That Will Change You and the
World Around You

**AG Hammersmith Publishing
2004**

This book is dedicated to my parents,
Joseph and Sylvia McGlothlin, who taught
these important lessons from my earliest days.

They are simply the best people I know.

CONTENTS

ACKNOWLEDGMENTS

I gratefully acknowledge and express deep appreciation to the many wonderful people who helped make this book possible:

To Becky Selfe for opening her life and sharing memories and homemade pumpkin pie. I hope I have painted a realistic and lasting picture of your husband and best friend.

To the entire Selfe family for welcoming me and sharing your undeniable strength and unending hospitality.

To my amazing parents Joseph and Sylvia McGlothlin for all your sacrifices over the years, the lessons you teach, and the love you give.

To my wonderful sisters Dyana McGlothlin Steely and Kathy McGlothlin Dotson, for your caring support and friendship.

To my beautiful nieces Kirsten Hylton, Kaycie Dotson and Connor Steely, for your bright smiles, little girl laughs and unconditional love.

To the gorgeous and brilliant Dr. Priya Patil for your love, passion, patience and holding my hand in the dark.

To my great friends Patrick Houghton, Tom O'Brian, Jonathan Cooper, Paul Overbay, Timothy Sams, Paul C. Harris, Ramesh Murthy, Peter Gretz, Tyler Sewell, Joe Cundiff, Matt Wilkinson, Michael S. Terry, Andrew Warren, Greg Warren, Apostolos Catsaros and Santiago Lluhi for your enduring wisdom and brotherhood.

To Emory and Henry College and all those who came before.

x

PREFACE

It is my sincere hope this book explains who and what Fred Selfe is and what he *can be* to our world. You did not have to know Fred Selfe, or of Emory and Henry College, to understand what his passing means to our entire culture: the loss of a good man, caring father, mentoring coach, guiding teacher; the loss of a true hero—one fewer of a quickly disappearing breed. It is my wish you find here the tools you need to become one of those real next-door heroes.

I also want to explain, if you did not attend Emory and Henry, it is not like your school. It is not the University of Virginia, Notre Dame, Duke or Michigan. It is not Rice, Tulane, Brown or Harvard. It is not Washington and Lee, Wake Forest, or Colby. Emory and Henry is a unique, small, beautiful, rural college where supernatural roots run deep into the ancient Appalachians anchoring it to the place it is built.

Those who go there share those roots—they grow in us, entangling us with the campus, its history and each other. They draw us back when the leaves of the hardwoods change to honey, fire and cumquat and sunlight passes through them like antique amber. The smells of mown grass, buttermilk fried chicken and Kentucky Bourbon drift along on the crisp midday air.

Cedar-stored wools, charcoal-colored flannels and worn earthen corduroy fold into the quilted backdrop of bright navy and golden flags shimmering in a pale washed sky. They remind us it is time for football and we are called to join our family at the great reunion.

Football season, the glorious autumn of the mountain empire of Southwestern Virginia, is the best time to learn this story; a time when bright colors envelope us and God's hand sweeps across the newly upturned fields bringing change to the world. A bold time is the best time to learn of Fred Selfe. He was the *uncle* in the Emory and Henry family—to some a father. His commanding presence on the football field and around campus, as he strode along in blue shorts and gray t-shirts, reassured us the college and its strength—of which we are a product— marched forward. He stood heads above others as the vintage–some might say *old-fashioned*—example of the solid, unwavering moral value of the institution. He *was* the things we need to be. If that is old fashioned, I say we need to slow down and find it again.

Enjoy this book and may you find in the life of Fred Selfe the lessons and tools you need to change your life and the world around you.

Dale McGlothlin
Greensboro, North Carolina

THE SELFE FACTOR

Fred Selfe Would Hate This Book

There is no doubt in my mind Coach Fred Dean Selfe would hate this book. I doubt he would even pick it up.

He did not like talking about himself, or being talked about. He was terrible at accepting acknowledgement or praise. God forbid you ever try to compliment him on anything to his face. It was like watching a man being chased by bees the way he would swing his hat around, put his hands on his hips and look up and down and all around.

He was an All-American football player, member of the college's Sports Hall of Fame, Old Dominion Athletic Conference Coach of the Year, and recipient of numerous awards for teaching and service. Yet, I am willing to wager he strongly disliked every second of receiving those honors—except maybe the All-American award for his play as an offensive lineman. He did not like drawing attention to himself for any reason.

For him the world was all about other folks.

Fred Selfe died January 24, 2003 from cancer. It was one of the few battles he ever lost. This book is inspired by him, about him, and—in a big way—for him. I played football for him as a fullback from 1983-1987, but more importantly spent the many years since understanding and accepting the importance of the simple, powerful lessons he taught me. My senior year we averaged a nationally-ranked 31.4 points per game, played in the NCAA playoffs, and produced three All Americans. He called us "a pretty dad-blasted tough team." Though he was the offensive coordinator who coached us to the national ranking, new rushing, passing and points-per-game records, and our 10-2 season he refused to take any credit for that success. He told a newspaper reporter that year, "I'm like any old dog who likes to get his head scratched, but [Head] Coach Wacker and the kids deserve the credit." But, truth be told, he was not like "any old dog." That selfless, serving attitude is one of the larger-than-life qualities that make him such a giant.

He was the living example of Emory and Henry College and its famed football program—one of the finest small college football programs in the country over the past half century. The school played against the University of Tennessee in the inaugural game of their first football stadium in 1921 and went on to become a national powerhouse during the war years of the 1940s. The "farm boys" of Emory and Henry played in the Tangerine Bowl in 1950 and 1951 when good football mattered more than ticket sales. In its long and venerable football tradition the college boasts 27 all-time conference championships and nine post season bowl games. Since 1982, Head Coach Lou Wacker's first year, the school won 11 Old Dominion Athletic Conference Championships, and played in five NCAA playoff games. The small, quiet, unassuming college program produced 37 All-Americans and an astounding 71.9 percent winning record.

Emory and Henry grows great coaches too. The college produces many high school and small college coaches, but also helps train men like Jim Grobe who coached there in the late 1970s and is now head coach at Wake Forest University. Coach Grobe is credited with turning the Demon Deacons' football program around and putting them squarely into the nation's top 25 teams.

Emory also gave Doug Blevins a start. Blevins, an Abingdon, Virginia native, came to E&H in 1984 as a kicking coach. Since then his resume boasts head kicking coach for the Miami Dolphins and kicking consultant for the Minnesota Vikings, New England Patriots, New York Jets and NFL Europe. Perhaps his most successful student is Adam Viniatieri, who kicked a last second field goal to win the Super Bowl for New England—*twice*—in 2002 *and* 2004. Coach Blevins' achievements are even more amazing when you consider he has the crippling condition cerebral palsy and has never walked a day in his life. His inspiring life has been profiled by *The New York Times*, *People*, *The Washington Post*, *Fast Company* and HBO's *Real Sports* with Bryant Gumbel.

The college even has a famous trick play set named for it— The *Emory and Henry Formation*. Steve Spurrier, while coaching the University of Florida, revived the "ole Emory and Henry shift" and pulled it out when he needed to completely confuse his SEC opponents—even had it used against him once by Western Michigan. Hundreds of thousands of football fans stared at their televisions in disbelief as the Gators shifted into *the Emory and Henry* on a critical third down against Alabama in the 1994 SEC Championship game. Quarterback Danny Wuerffel took full advantage of the confused Crimson Tide to gain a crucial first down that gave the momentum back to Florida. They marched down the field to win the game 24-23. Spurrier, who grew up in Johnson City, Tennessee, says he became a fan of the formation watching E&H games in the 1950s. Dave Kindred, a writer for *The Sporting News*, describes the *Emory and Henry Formation* like this: "To see the oddly gapped spread formation is to be dumbfounded. It looks like 11 guys who got lost on the way to the huddle. There's a center with a guard on either side. Behind them are the quarterback and a running back. The tackles are split 15 yards wide with ends beside them and a receiver behind them."

Spurrier introduced the formation to the NFL coaching the Washington Redskins in 2001 and it has since been used by the Tennessee Titans and Buffalo Bills.

I once heard E&H's football program rightly described as *"good old-fashioned, smash-mouth football"*—no scholarships, no big endorsement deals, and no massive stadiums—just young athletes playing for the love of the game in a small, simple, tree-lined stadium overflowing with waves of blue and gold clad alumni cheering them on. It is the same for the highly successful basketball team—and baseball team, tennis team, track team, volleyball team, soccer team and on and on. Small college sports with big time heart and soul.

That extra heart comes as payment-in-kind for the opportunity the college offers young men and women. A former student observed Fred Selfe addressing a student-athletic faculty committee and notes how the coach defined his personal understanding of the role of college athletics: "To teach athletes positive virtues on the field and to allow young people who might otherwise never go to college encounter life-changing thoughts and ideas in the classroom. They may come because they are players, but we want them to leave having become scholars."

Emory and Henry is a small liberal arts college in the classic tradition of schools created in the late 1700s and early 1800s to enlighten and educate the sons and daughters of the young country's first pioneers. It is a postcard picture of a Southern college with neatly groomed green commons, flowering beds overflowing with yellows and whites, brown bracken-ringed ponds reflecting weeping willows and dirty white geese, and red-orange brick buildings whispering forgotten stories of the Civil War. Founded by concerned religious and education leaders, it served as an important institution of learning as these intrepid people pushed westward over the Blue Ridge Mountains into the great unknown of our new country.

Early Virginia pioneers left the safety of Williamsburg, Richmond, and Charlottesville to journey headlong into the undiscovered. What today takes six or seven hours by car was then the great unknown area listed on early colonial maps simply as "plentiful hunting and trapping." It was America's earliest frontier attracting stout, individualistic men and women willing to hunt, dig and scratch out an existence from a true wilderness.

Extreme Southwestern Virginia is an area perhaps best known for being *unknown*. It quietly sits in the extreme western reaches of a state that once stretched from shore to shore of this unexplored country. Here Virginia's tallest mountains jut up from the neatly cultivated fields like giant dragon's teeth eating the world from within. These mountains that surround the college are the ignored younger sibling of the famous Smokies to the west and the rugged Cohuttas to the south—a Cherokee word meaning *poles of the shed* as these indigenous peoples believed the peaks held up the very sky. The mountains that ring my college are known, or unknown as it seems, by less ambitious names like White Top, Iron and Pond. Even Virginia's highest point, Mount Rogers at 5,729 feet, which can be seen from almost every entrance to the college, gets little respect and is named for an obscure professor from the University of Virginia some 250 road miles to the north.

Emory and Henry sits quietly tucked away in a fertile agricultural valley at the center of the area Teddy Roosevelt once called a "wild border democracy." It was founded in 1838 by descendents of those brave pioneers who needed to keep their sons close to the farm. It has the distinction of being the first institution of higher learning west of the main Blue Ridge Mountains and is squarely in the path of the second frontier—whatever lay over and beyond the very edge of the 18th Century American experience—the original gateway to America's West—the great Cumberland Gap. Fred Selfe was a son of these mountains and this "wild border democracy" was the ideal place to attract and train his scholar-athletes.

The "Gentle Colossus"

In all my travels, experiences and encounters Fred Selfe is still one of the most extraordinary people I have the privilege of knowing. He was a tall, exceptionally strong and athletic man. He was quiet and humble. He worked hard and rarely showed fatigue. The Reverend David St. Clair referred to him as a "gentle colossus." Since his childhood in the small town of Castlewood, Virginia, Fred

Selfe lived a good life serving others without thoughts of reward or praise. He spent his youth in the fields, was the valedictorian of his high school class, played every musical instrument except the flute and drums, and spent his college summers doing the work of three people unloading freight in the nearby town of Abingdon.

He was vintage—*old school*—a throwback to simpler days—a solid rock of unchanging values.

He played on the Emory and Henry football and baseball teams and excelled at both—starting every game of his four years achieving All-American honors as an offensive lineman. He graduated from Emory and Henry in 1969 with a B.S. in economics then received his M.A. from East Tennessee State University before coming back to Emory as an assistant football coach.

He was a loyal husband. He and wife Becky Selfe, an equally dedicated teacher and track coach, were quietly married her senior year in high school—his freshman year in college. He hitchhiked over 100 miles every weekend to be with her. She remained the love of his life and he referred to her as "my bride" for 38 years. He was a loving, encouraging, sometimes overly-protective father to their only child, Paige, and fell over himself being the doting grandfather to Paige's children, Samantha and Fred Jr. All of this may make him seem a normal, average man who loved his job, wife and family, but as you read this book you will find he was so much more. *He was extraordinary in a world of average.*

His friend, coaching colleague, former Ranger platoon leader with the 101st Airborne Division and decorated Vietnam War veteran, Bob Johnson says through his experiences he has known many fine men, "some of whom are buried in Arlington." Johnson's father, Gen. Harold K. Johnson, served as President Lyndon Johnson's Army Chief of Staff during a crucial period of the war in Vietnam. Yet, Bob Johnson calls Fred Selfe *the best man I ever knew.*

So many people across our country, from Los Angeles to Rhode Island, feel the same about this exceptional man; a man who lived simply, served his community, coached the college's Division III football and baseball teams, and shaped the lives of countless men and women. As Tom Fletcher, a former assistant football coach at Virginia Tech, the University of Virginia, and the University of North Carolina told a *Roanoke Times* newspaper, "In my lifetime, with all the people I've been associated with, he absolutely stands among the top people. He was just a wonderful person."

Fred Selfe lived his life with the important principles most of us lack. He did small things that took root in the hearts and minds of those who witnessed them and shaped us in lasting ways. These small acts of kindness, courage, consistency, character, strength, poise, compassion, and selflessness become great big things in our timid, tepid world. In one of his missives on leadership, Harvard professor Joseph L. Badaracco, Jr. quotes business executive and former U.S. Congressman Bruce Barton: "Sometimes, when I consider what tremendous consequences come from little things—a chance word, a tap on the shoulder, or a penny dropped on a newsstand— I am tempted to think *there are no little things*."

I agree with Mr. Barton. I also agree with Bob Johnson when he says it is difficult—sometimes heart-wrenching and hand-wringing—to talk about Fred Selfe because, "He died unexpectedly—too soon—*while we still need him*." I firmly believe our families, schools, communities, cities and our country need Fred Selfe and people like him—people who do *Great Big Small Things* each day just because they are the right things. We should honor them and learn from their actions. People should have clamored for Fred Selfe's autograph and erected statues of him in public places for the all good he did. It would have irked him to no end to pass by a towering image of his own likeness, and he would have fought it every step of the way, but it is what should be.

Crowfoot, a warrior of the Blackfoot tribe, described the kind of life Fred Selfe lived with his dying words in 1890, "*What is life?*" *It is the flash of a firefly in the night. It is the breath of a buffalo in the wintertime. It is the little shadow which runs across the grass and loses itself in the sunset*." These are images of simplicity, strength and beauty—images that remain in the mind's eye when the event is long over. Living things go on forever. Fred Selfe's life continues through the small things—the *Great Big Small Things*.

The Power of Small Things

Each day the small things he did for others are repeated by those he touched and those small things get bigger. Steve "Monk" Munsey tells this story of a small thing Fred Selfe did to touch his life in a big way: "When I finished my final year of football, Coach Selfe took my helmet on equipment day, looked at it then handed it back to me. He said, '*Monk, there's a crack in this helmet. It's not fit for us to keep. You take it.*' He knew how much a silly old football helmet would mean to a simple country boy like me. That helmet is my pride and joy. I think Fred knew how my days at Emory—including the times spent under his life teachings—would live on through that helmet. Just the way Coach Selfe will live on through us. And to this day, I've never found the crack in that helmet."

Pat Walker, a *Wasp* football player in the early 1990s and current assistant football coach at North Carolina Wesleyan College, calls Coach Selfe the "closest thing to a father" he ever had. Walker tells how Fred Selfe cared for "an underachiever;" guiding him into the teaching profession in which he now excels. "I saw him the summer before his last year of life," Walker recalls, "He knew he was sick and didn't tell me. I had my two boys with me (my third son was born two weeks before he died) and he played with them while we visited. Before we left, he took off his old beat up baseball cap, put it on my head and told me he wanted me to have it. So, not only do I have the lessons he taught me and the great memories we shared, but I guess he wanted me to have something tangible as well. He didn't have to do that, but God knows how grateful I am he did."

Each day someone uses a principle in their own life they learned and embraced from observing him. Someone asks what Fred Selfe would do in a certain situation. Someone teaches someone else a lesson they learned from him. Someone stops to help a stranded motorist, shovels snow from the driveway of a neighbor, gives a few dollars to a needy stranger, or a beaten up old baseball cap or football helmet to a young man or woman who will cherish it forever. Each day someone *is* Fred Selfe.

Allyson Cox Newton, a teacher and E&H graduate, writes in a personal letter: "Not a week goes by that I am not reminded of something you said or did . . . or how you handled a situation that makes me stop, think and then—hopefully—make the right decision." Newton describes Coach Selfe as "big in stature, big in compassion, big in heart with a constant warm twinkle . . . ." She also admits, "When I was in college and for all the years after I would tell my family that 'one of these days I am going to marry Coach Selfe!' My parents, chuckling, would remind me that I would first have to talk to Mrs. Selfe and Paige. I would reply, 'Well, I will just have to marry someone *like* Coach Selfe.' I hope one day I will have an impact on a few of my students like you had on many of yours."

Steve Allen, a lightning-fast receiver who played football for Emory and Henry in the early 1980s, is now head football coach at Flagler Palm Coast High School in Bunnell, Florida. Steve sums up Fred Selfe's indelible influence in a letter to Becky Selfe: "Without having known Coach Selfe, I would never have been a coach. Heck, I might be digging ditches somewhere! He was a tremendous role model. He looked after me when I didn't even know I needed to be cared for. He supported me when I didn't support him. He taught me although I was not ready to learn. Most of all he showed me how to conduct myself as a young man when I was just a boy."

This book is not a biography of Fred Selfe, instead it is a collection of stories and lessons of the amazingly good things Fred Selfe did for the world and an awestruck appreciation for what they will continue to do.

I include a very personal narrative in the book's epilogue of Fred Selfe's memorial service and how we celebrated his life that day. You may choose to read it first—if so, I hope it serves as an introduction to the man and the college—an explanation of what leads me to write this book and sows the seeds of the *Selfe Factor*. The second epilogue is a remembrance of Fred Selfe by Emory and Henry's 18th president, Dr. Charles Sydnor. Dr. Sydnor's essay is also a wonderful portrait of the coach and the college.

Chapter one explains how small things get to be great big things that change the world around us. Chapters two through nine are the lessons—Fred Selfe's *Great Big Small Things*—you can use to change your life. These chapters describe:

1. **Why we need the *Great Big Small Thing***

2. **How Fred Selfe defined it**

3. **How you can use the *Great Big Small Thing* in your life**

Through the memories of those who knew him it weaves a colorful story of his amazing character and recognizes the powerful virtues and lessons he left to inspire and change us—lessons that, if enough people learn and share with others, can help rebuild our fractured culture.

I know as you read this book Fred Selfe is somewhere up there, shaking his head, swatting away with his blue and gold baseball cap, and with that stern look on his face telling no one in particular, "*Gosh dandy! Bullfrog youngun!*" But, he never did like talking about what to do—he just liked doing it.

Forget all the best-selling self-help books, workshops for dummies, and extension classes. Forget the *Leadership Secrets of* books, and the big name speakers who charge thousands of dollars for a weekend of showbiz. If you are searching for a real life example for doing better as a person, parent, teacher, coach, manager—or if you just wake up each morning and do not see the person in the mirror you want to see—read this book. Fred Selfe lived a life full of examples and taught powerful lessons of being and doing *Great Big Small Things* for others. He was a teacher of exceptional skill and I am determined to define and explain how the principles by which he lived and those he displayed every day are the principles that make us all good people. Ensuring those lessons does not end with his death, but continue through the chronicling of his life.

Use the life of Fred Selfe to mold and change your own life. Begin the process of making yourself into a better person. Do Fred Selfe's *Great Big Small Things* each day to make the world a better place.

FIRST GREAT BIG SMALL THING

There Are No Small Things

As iron sharpens iron, so one man sharpens another.

Proverbs 27:17

I firmly believe one person can change the world. This ancient belief has become a prominent principle of our modern Chaos Theory known as the *butterfly effect*. Edward Lorenz, the man who coined the phrase in the 1970s, describes the effect by using an example of tiny air disturbances from the flapping of a butterfly's wings in Brazil ultimately leading to a dramatic storm in far away Texas. The action of the small wings changes the entire complex weather system. Unlike the *domino theory* in which each falling domino merely replicates an effect, the *butterfly effect* amplifies the condition each time it occurs until it becomes as large as a tornado. The beating of the small, delicate wings disrupts and changes the complex system in an exponential way.

To think an assistant football coach at a small country college can have positively touched millions of people around our country by the standard of his own life is an ideal example of the butterfly effect at work. The appreciation and imitation of Fred Selfe's life and principles is the model of the great exponential force of something seemingly small in action. One good person doing small things can change everything else in our world. It is proof our cultural decline is not irreversible. I believe the small things—the simple lessons of Fred Selfe's life and their butterfly effect are just the sort of storm we need.

Fred Selfe was a man who made the world about other people. He taught, coached and worked for others, though during his lifetime he may not have known exactly how awesome and far-reaching were his actions. He helped build houses for the poor, shoveled snow for the elderly, chopped and delivered wood to those who would go cold without it, mentored young men and women who had no fathers of their own, gave money to people who had none, cared for the sick, and pitched in to help families move to new homes. He did all this and much more with absolutely no regard for reward or even appreciation.

He was a man who lived a life of integrity—a life that touched so many others in strong and permanent ways. The people he affected continue to spread those small things to others each day through their lives and works. He was this way his entire life. As he claimed in a 1986 newspaper interview, "People who know me know I've had the same haircut for thirty years . . . that I rarely change." That lasting quality is what those who knew him in college in the late 1960s share with those who met him for the first time in 2003 just before he died. You will share it too when you read this book.

I thoroughly believe the lessons of Fred Selfe's character can stanch the outflow of our traditional culture and, I boldly assert, offer us the tools for its rebuilding. Like the tiny butterfly's wings, one person can change our culture. If you read this and pause, perhaps doubt what the authors of the best-selling business book, *Built to Last*, James Collins and Jerry Porras call my *BHAG—big hairy, audacious goal*—I offer this:

> Coach Selfe coached an average 150 people (football, baseball) each year for 26 years. That equals 3,900 people directly affected by his life and teaching.

> If only 33 percent of those people were affected enough to emulate him, then 1,287 people exhibit the same traits.

> If those people coach, teach, manage or lead 100 people a year using the same teaching style that equals 128,700 people a year, multiplied by 26 years equals 3,346,200 people.

There are 3.3 million men and women touched by the life of one simple man at a small college in a rural Southern town. It is the best example I know of the Biblical proverb, *"As iron sharpens iron, so one man sharpens another."* This man of iron has sharpened a group of men and women who use his lessons to sharpen others, and in turn, sharpen our culture.

What can you do to begin the honing process?

ONE GREAT BIG SMALL THING

1)   As *Iron Sharpens Iron*, Your Life Can Sharpen So Many Others

Read this book about Fred Selfe's life and deeds and use it to change your life. Imagine how many people you can touch: family, friends, business colleagues, students, partners, employees, players—heck—people you meet on the street, on airplanes or in elevators. It reminds me of the movie *Pay it Forward* in which an 11-year-old boy, in response to a challenge by his teacher, proposes an idea for individual deeds to change the world. The life of one good person can change a family, neighborhood, school, town, city, state and country *if* you do something good for someone else and *they* pass it on.

Mark Jones played for the *Wasps* in the late 1980s and claims Fred Selfe's care and concern shaped his life and continues to move him each day: "I went through some personal problems during my junior year and for the first three months of the new school year I left Emory. I needed to get myself straightened out, so I went home to Shallotte to work for a year. While I was away, Coach Selfe called time and again to see how I was doing. He eventually convinced me to come back to Emory and get my degree. I am glad I listened to him." Jones is head football and softball coach, Athletic Director, and Teacher of the Year (2002) at Shallotte Middle School in Shallotte, North Carolina. Jones goes on to say it was a remarkable thing for Emory and Henry's offensive coordinator to take such a personal interest in him because he was not even on the offensive team. He was, instead, a *defensive player*—an outside linebacker on the "red team that scrimmaged against the first and second team offense and ran the opponent's defensive schemes week after week." He says Fred Selfe's ability to make even third and fourth string players feel special made all the difference in his life and is something he practices as a coach: "I don't know where I'd be if Coach Selfe hadn't talked me into coming back to Emory and getting my degree. There are people on this earth who have the gift of making other people feel good—Coach Selfe had that gift. I know there is a big place in Heaven for him because he was so good to so many people."

Phillip Henley, head football coach at Lebanon High School, in Lebanon, Virginia played baseball and football for Fred Selfe and agrees with Jones: "As a high school football coach and administrator there are countless lessons Coach Selfe instilled in me that I apply on a daily basis: win and lose with dignity; be fair and honest to my players and students; respect my opponents; gain and give respect to my players and, most importantly, to respect myself as a educator. In my office I have a picture of Coach Selfe hanging on the wall so all students, players, coaches, and faculty who enter may see the person I most respect, honor, and call my friend. If I can be only half the coach and man he was I will be eternally grateful."

Steve Munsey tells this story about the most important lesson he learned from his coach: "Football players at E&H love to *go live*—it is game situation, with full contact until the whistle blows. As a cornerback, I was serving as the right 'end rusher' on the goal line defense. This particular drill was for the defense to work on blocking extra points and field goals. The kicker was unavailable at the time, so Coach Selfe stood in as the kicker. I recall making a statement along the lines of, 'Watch out Coach Selfe, we're going live!' His response was something like, 'Yes, you better,' with that well-known grin on his face. On the snap, the football squirmed out of the holder's hands. *Live ball*! As I sped full-bore to recover the muffed snap, a powerful block stopped me—lifted me off the ground several inches and pitched me backward. As I came back down flailing there was Coach Selfe, crouched, his sun-glassed face inches from my facemask, arms cocked back like hammers on a double barrel shotgun, ready for another convincing strike. I quickly let him know one *chuck* from him was enough and I put my arms up in surrender. I told that story many times to fellow students and the new friends I made since graduating from E&H. I always told the story in a way that revealed Coach Selfe's physical power and size . . . how he could have easily leveled me with another chuck. Until recently I did not realize I was missing the point. The lesson is—like Coach Selfe's participation in a live football drill with no pads, no helmet, no mouthpiece, no cleats—when you choose to become part of something, whether it is accepting employment or giving your word, you do so completely and without reservation. His involvement in the drill revealed that whether prepared for the situation or not, when you raise your hand to accept responsibilities, you give the most you can, not the least you can get away with. In other words, you always *go live* in life's decisions. I understand and try to follow the example of responsibility he gave me that day, which further supported what my parents had instilled in me early in my life. Though I will probably often fail at living up to Coach Selfe's example, the lesson he taught will never fail me."

These stories, and the ones that follow, affirm my belief in another important scientific tenet—*The First Law of Thermodynamics*. This law, also called the Law of

Conservation of Mass and Energy, is called a "law" because within the bounds of scientific observation it has been proven true beyond all reasonable doubt. It states that matter and energy cannot be created nor can it be destroyed—only changed and modified. Matter—the basis of everything animate and inanimate on this planet—cannot end. Mankind cannot create new matter; neither can mankind fully destroy matter. We can change burn it, explode it, freeze it, and smash it, but we cannot make it go away—only change into a new form.

For me, this *scientific* law proves two things I never doubted: First, there is a God and He created all things—we humans can neither create nor destroy matter. It exists and we had nothing to do with it. Only an intelligent superior being can create matter and shape it to work in such intricate, mathematically improbable ways. Secondly, it proves Fred Selfe's life force—his will and character—did not go away.

According to the First Law of Thermodynamics it cannot go away. His life continues and becomes something new again each day through those he touched—it changes into something new with each person who uses these lessons and passes them on to another. His nine simple, yet essential lessons will help us progress into a better, stronger, and more morally sustainable future *if* we own them and go out and share them with others.

SECOND GREAT BIG SMALL THING

A Culture in Peril: Why We Need Fred Selfe Now More Than Ever

Ya gotta admire the Chinese. They've seen the fork and they're still going with the chopsticks.

Jerry Seinfeld

Perhaps I am just getting older, but conversation at parties has turned from safe, innocuous subjects like sports, movies and music to the weighty topic of the decline of our American culture. At every cookout, birthday party, dinner party, and Arbor Day celebration I attend these days, as soon as the obligatory "*how is work*" question is out of the way we rush headlong into the most recent murderous spree splayed across the front page of our newspapers, the shock of the latest eight-year-old we saw dressed like Britney Spears, drug raids at the local high school, or the lawsuit by the 56-year-old, obese Bronx man against Burger King, McDonalds, Wendy's and KFC because their food *made* him weigh 270 pounds and have a heart attack.

In these conversations I find myself with clinched jaw enthusiastically nodding affirmations while my friends gathered around the mini-quiche tray slosh red wine from their glasses dramatically recounting the failures of a culture where 25 percent of all newborns have no official father, suicide is the third leading cause of death among young people ages 15 to 24, and 1.9 million people are locked away in jails and prisons.

Sociologists point with alarm to the red-line indicators of the health of a culture—violent crime, educational system, births to single parents, alcohol and drug abuse, suicide rate, etc. These statistics show, while we are still running the race, we exhibit symptoms of diseases that attack us from the inside. I believe the diseases are identifiable and curable.

The first of the diseases we contracted is a lack of personal courage. We are becoming a culture devoid of the courage it takes to stand up for what is right; to speak out against what we know is wrong; to roll up our sleeves to work for needed change. Courage shows up least in the places we need it most: our families, neighborhoods, churches and synagogues, businesses, schools, and other institutions of civil society.

Another of our maladies is a loss of community. We care less about our fellow humans. We are less societal; we trust less; we cocoon inside our homes and give less money to local non-profit entities like the United Way and Lion's Club. We disengage from our community and hide in the gray area of moral, cognitive, aesthetic, and cultural relativism; the *shadowland* between right and wrong.

The last infection that threatens to end the life of our culture is a severe deficiency of good leaders. Although I am no sociologist, it may be correlative our vanishing sense of community and subsequent loss of trust coincides with a shortage of good leaders in our towns, clubs and organizations, schools, governments, and workplaces.

Taken separately these losses are lamentable—things people talk about in bars and on airplane trips between free peanuts and the start of the movie. Together, though, courage, community and good leadership form the backbone of our traditional American culture and without them we cannot stand upright in a time when nothing is as it was: We are running out of oil; China controls the global economy; France and Germany are working *together*, at our expense, to control a united Europe; Muslims are uniting to form "Islamic democracies" that smack of a new form of repressive fascism the likes of which we fought, bled and died to defeat in the 1940s; terrorists of diverse nationalities and ideologies—splinter groups from the same piece of rotting wood—band together under the banner of al-Qaeda for a global *jihad* aimed mainly at us. Externally the world is more dangerous for our country and our national interests than the day when we had thousands of Soviet missiles pointed at our major population centers.

Internally, we face a country divided. Political entities have used our differences to drive wedges into our society—pitting rich against poor, workers against corporations, black against Hispanic, white against black, Hispanic against white, and on and on. These forces have worked for many years to divide us for their own personal and political gain. Race warfare, class warfare, sex warfare—these short-sighted people light the dry wood of discord wherever they uncover it. The flames of our own destruction are fanned by our fiddling around fighting each other.

As the old proverb says, "If we do not change the direction we are going, we are likely to end up where we are headed."

Courage

Personal courage is rarely the most convenient thing to do. It is choosing a side when others straddle the fence. It is speaking out when others sit on their hands. It is as simple as getting up to do something because it need be done while others sit around and talk about it. I once asked U.S. Senator George Allen when he was serving as Governor of Virginia if he minded being hounded and attacked by the opposition at every step. He laughed aloud and explained, "You have to take a side, and when you do, you are automatically upsetting 50 percent of the people who care about that issue." Exhibiting personal courage will create controversy and stir resentment, but, it is a virtue worth possessing—more than any amount of gold or silver.

You may equate personal courage with Rosa Parks refusing to give up her seat, or the lone man holding only a shopping bag stopping a column of tanks heading to massacre students in Tiananmen Square, and you would be right. But, the courage to do what needs be done can be simpler and closer to home. It can be the courage to speak out at a school meeting and take the unpopular side of an issue; to run for public office; to stop and help someone carry groceries or fix a flat even though you'll be late for an appointment, or show tough love to a child. Personal courage is doing what must be done regardless of what others do or what obstacles stand in the way. Courage also means turning away from doing the wrong thing.

Have you not heard this question asked time and again, "What if the average German citizen had stood up to the small Nazi party early in the 1920s?" How different would our world be today? Let me ask it again using different times and antagonists. What would the world be if someone had stopped Pol Pot's Khmer Rouge movement in the early 1970s? What if someone had reported Eric Harris and Dylan Klebold before the 1999 shooting spree at Columbine High School? What if *someone* had done *something*? The *what-ifs* keep those of us who care deeply about our and our neighbor's futures awake long into the night.

There is a story from India about a mouse afraid of cats. A magician comes along and agrees to turn the mouse into a cat. Soon, though, the mouse-turned-cat calls for the magician. He has met a dog and is once again afraid. So, the magician turns him into a dog. The mouse-turned-cat-turned-dog is content until he meets a tiger. Again the magician turns him into what he fears. Finally, however, when the tiger meets a hunter the magician refuses to help and turns him back into a mouse explaining, "For though you have the body of a tiger you still have the heart of a mouse."

How many of us today make ourselves into tigers, but still have the heart of a mouse? How often do you pick up a stranger's burden? How often do you stand up when all those around you sit still? How often do you turn away from the wrong thing?

Community

In his book, *Bowling Alone*, Robert Putnam, a Harvard professor of public policy, describes how we have become increasingly disconnected from family, friends, neighbors, and our democratic structures and the ill-effects on our lives and communities. Putnam uses nearly 500,000 interviews over 25 years to show we "sign fewer petitions, belong to fewer organizations that meet, know our neighbors less, meet with friends less frequently, and even socialize with our families less often." More Americans are bowling than ever before, but we are not bowling in leagues—we are *bowling alone.*

I remember my grandmother, Flora French, who passed away a few years ago at 92 years of age, saying to me many times while I was a kid running around the gnarled apple trees in her yard, "Son, we were better off during the Great Depression." When I eventually asked what she meant, she explained during the worst economic disaster in our country's history her entire neighborhood banded together to help one another. "If one person didn't have food, the rest of us would pitch in a little and take it to them." They knew who lived where, how much food they had, who was employed and who was not, and when anyone was sick. They knew and cared for each other because they shared a neighborhood.

That neighborhood was her world. Even after the stroke that would eventually end her life she walked up and down those sidewalks visiting the few friends who remained. Families moved, people died, new families moved in and everything was different. Now, she knew almost no one on the street where she spent most of her life and that saddened her. No one came by to introduce themselves; no one stopped to talk when she sat on her front porch; no one had lawn parties or shared gardens. She felt we lost our sense of neighborhood. There was no one to bring food to those who had too little, or help tend to the sick, or even to sit for a while on the front porch with the lonely older people whose spouses had passed.

Her neighborhood disappeared around her and, though the houses were still there, the *community* was gone. She decried for many years what sociologists are finally discovering today; we have lost our sense of community and with it the implicit covenant of knowing, interacting with and helping the folks around us.

Many, like Robert Putnam, believe the loss of community a precursor to the decline of our entire culture. Without it we feel alone, isolated and disconnected. This solitude breeds hopelessness and with it our instances of crime, divorce, alcoholism and drug addiction—factors political scientist Francis Fukuyama calls our "social dysfunctions," rise at alarming rates. These dysfunctions are eroding the great foundation on which our country and, subsequently, our culture are built; democracy.

Our traditional society clustered in neighborhoods like my grandmother's *Brooklyn Addition*. German sociologist, Juergen Habermas, theorizes our personal neighborhoods, ethnic communities, churches, cities, towns, and families as the very "lifeworlds" in which our personal form of democracy exists; the place where we interact and conduct civic activity; where we practice and foster the ideals of equality and responsibility. If our *lifeworlds* are shrinking, does that mean our democracy is vanishing? And if our democracy—the very foundation of John Winthrop's "city upon a hill"—is disappearing, how long can our culture stand on the shifting sands?

What I understand from my work and travel around this country is our communities, our *lifeworlds*, are made up of the people who inhabit these worlds; their personal characters form the concrete that binds us together. Our neighbors are the colorful threads that make up the patchwork quilt that is America. They are the people whose actions, or inactions in our current state, decide in which direction the culture goes; forward, in neutral, or backwards toward the same mistakes we made in the not-so-glorious past. Here, I assert, is where courage and community co-join. They are the double helix of our cultural DNA.

Leadership

Our nation is experiencing a scarcity of good leadership. By *good leaders* I mean people who exhibit traditional qualities of successful leadership: accept the responsibility of being a leader, serve others, stay grounded, focus on the mission, communicate well, listen well, challenge others, manage anxiety, treat others with respect, exhibit deep concern for others, reward top performers, encourage discipline, and personally exemplify all of these traits through the actual practice of them.

Good leaders are followed, imitated and admired not because they talk about these traits, but because they *are* these traits. They are walking examples of leadership.

Today's heroes are sports stars, entertainment celebrities, and musicians. Not to say some of these people are not good leaders, but on the whole, they are admired not for their leadership qualities, but for their athletic prowess, *up yours* attitude, acting ability, or material wealth they possess. They are, for the most part, not *good leaders* as defined by the traits I listed. People look up to, dress like, walk and talk like these *de facto* icons because we *do not* have the sort of immediate civic leadership we used to admire. Too few are the town councilors, mayors, governors, or congressmen without personal blemish; the patient Little League coach, the pious priest; the servant minister or rabbi; the parent who parents instead of buddies; the Peace Corps volunteer who teaches; the honest CEO; the energetic teacher.

Strange how these once stereotypical roles have become some of our rarest sightings. But in a time when more people believe in the existence of UFOs than believe they will ever see money from the U.S. Social Security System, perhaps it is not all that odd. Our trust in government, organizations, clubs, corporations, and even our fellow humans is at an all time low.

We perceive these important positions of leadership filled by their opposites. We live in such times as these: a recent National Review Board study shows 4,392 Catholic clergymen involved in the sexual abuse of over 10,000 children; Peace Corps volunteerism dropped so dramatically we had to create a paid volunteer program called AmeriCorps; CEOs of WorldCom, HealthSouth, ImClone, Tyco, and Enron—to name only a few—bilked shareholders out of hundreds of millions and employee pension funds out of billions; *Education Week* magazine revealed 20 percent of new teachers leave the classroom after three years, and 50 percent quit after five years—at a time when we expect to need two million new teachers by 2011; Harris, Pew, *Wall Street Journal*/NBC, ABC and *Washington Post* polls over the past 30 years show campaign promises regarding cutting taxes, whether made by Republicans or Democrats, have little to no credibility.

I do not want these examples to overshadow the fact we do have some good leaders in our neighborhoods and towns; but we certainly have fewer than ever. One thing I can tell you from my personal experiences working with large U.S. companies, when there are no good leaders the ship sails without course and many times into dangerous waters. We need to build a new generation of leaders in all aspects of our civil and social society.

This backward leap into moral peril is more noticeable because it is constantly juxtaposed with media stories of the *phenomenal* progress in the material areas of our society; the things science and marketers claim will save us—from work, diseases, yellowing teeth, menopause, less than 40 miles-per-gallon, food that takes longer than a minute to prepare, or the stress of taking longer than a minute to get on the Internet.

As I write this we have two robotic vehicles rolling across the surface of Mars beaming pictures back to a NASA website for all to view; South Korean researchers cloned a human embryo and extracted stem cells; I point my mobile phone at a frog with three heads, snap a digital picture and instantly send it to my sister in Williamsburg; I stand on a conference room floor in Orlando, Florida handwriting notes on the screen of a handheld tablet PC and wirelessly send the information directly to a manufacturer in Bangalore, India. We have drugs that level out chemical imbalances, send tiny seeds of radiation into cancerous tumors to fight it from the inside, and promote erections that last up to four hours. All wondrous things that delight and entertain us; make our lives easier and give us the ability to do things we have never done.

We wake up each day to learn of the creation or innovation of, what was yesterday, merely a dream. Certainly it adds to our bank vault overflowing with national ego, but what does it do for our country's social and moral capital? I believe if we were to check our balance on that account, we would find ourselves close to bankruptcy.

These marvels of our own genius are not just seen once on Sunday over coffee in the *New York Times*, but every 15 minutes of our day on CNN's *Headline News* as we eat our cereal, every website we come across once we reach the office, the television conveniently placed in the dentist's office, the subway going home, the back of the seat on a flight across the country, and delivered to us via text messaging on our PDAs and mobile phones while we're in the bathroom. We are covered in this news sludge from the time the sun rises until it hurries around to rise again.

What Are You Doing

Perhaps our unique *American-ness* makes us feel good to be in a society moving at light speed. We are so accustomed to being number one and far out ahead of the rest of the world we have stopped looking forward and now sit admiring our images in the mirror; however, "objects in the rear view mirror may be closer than they appear." The traditions that made our culture the strongest in the history of the world are still with us, just far behind us in the dust of our passing—obscured by the false belief the advancement of technology means the advancement of the culture.

We Americans wear pants that repel moisture through nanotechnology as we pump fuel made from corn into our cars with GPS, while our kids watch DVDs on the plasma screens that pop out of the vehicle's ceiling. So, we pat ourselves on the back because, as we are told, we are making progress. But what if this material "progress" is really just shiny new vinyl siding we nailed over the rusted out hull of our culture? While Moore's Law may be ideal for measuring the advancement of semiconductor chips, we do a poor job measuring cultural development. Sure, we have the models of Piaget, Loevinger, Kegan, and Kohlberg, but we sorely lack a unified scale of individual and collective development that takes into account all it means to be human. The progress of our cultural development cannot possibly be understood by simply measuring economic or political terms.

Of the many friends and acquaintances I have from California to Virginia and New York to Texas, I cannot name more than two people who do not believe our culture is heading in the wrong direction. Most believe we are experiencing a cultural *regression*—we are literally moving backwards and devolving culturally.

Bill Bennett, former U.S. Secretary of Education, wrote about this incongruence as far back as 1993:

> Since 1960, the U.S. population has increased 41 percent; the GDP has nearly tripled; and social spending...has risen from $143.73 billion to $787 billion. Inflation-adjusted spending on welfare has increased by 630 percent and spending on education by 225 percent.

> But during the same 30 year period there has been a 560 percent increase in violent crime; a 419 percent increase in illegitimate births; a quadrupling in divorce rates; a tripling of the percentage of children living in single-parent homes; more than a 200 percent increase in the teenage suicide rate; and a drop of almost 80 points in SAT scores.

So, my answer to people I meet at these parties, over the neatly arranged cheese tray as our cultural decline is discussed, is simply this, "So, what are *you* doing about it?" This question usually stops a good piece of Vermont White Cheddar in mid-bite. However, I believe it is the most pertinent question we can ask in this age of indifference. For tomorrow, when our economy is void of manufacturing jobs and the equipment to manufacture anything even if we wanted; when we buy Chinese-branded cars and mobile phones; when we have lost our dominance in the world, and relevant-democracy rules in places where only certain religions are allowed and representatives are not directly elected, we will look back and wonder why no one did anything to stop it.

What if we lose our community, personal courage and good leadership? How far are we from the complete disintegration of our country? Can a sovereign country sustain democracy when more than half of eligible voters don't go to the polls, or does that country fall to the autocratic forces that wait in the shadows for the vacuum created when we abdicate responsibilities, take our liberties for granted, and sit on our hands. "Why didn't I do something?" will be the banal regret repeated as we look upon our ruinous city upon a hill, as we now look at the remains of the ancient empires of Sparta, Greece, Rome, and Byzantium; fields of tumbled stones and forgotten names. It will echo as the collective slogan of our Promethean culture as the embers die and the warmth recedes.

TWO GREAT BIG SMALL THINGS

1) *As Iron Sharpens Iron*, Your Life Can Sharpen So Many Others
2) Beat Your Wings

As I said in the last chapter, the *butterfly effect* of a good life can make for a storm that can change the face of the earth. You must remember Fred Selfe was a simple man at a small college in a rural Southern town. If he helped millions of people in his too-short life there is a great chance you can do the same. A small trickle of water can carve the deepest cavern if it continues to flow each and every day. Even if you do not reach *millions*, would it hurt to help thousands, or hundreds, or even one other person? What if your life makes one other person's life better? Would you consider your life worthwhile if as the Emerson poem says you, "leave the world a bit better, whether by a healthy child, a garden patch or a redeemed social condition; to know even one life has breathed easier because you have lived . . . ?"

Linda Williams Wiseman, a teacher in Floyd County, Virginia and former *Wasp* volleyball and basketball star, says she was influenced by Fred Selfe as coach, teacher, and a truly caring man. She explains it only took a small act, a remembrance, a kind word to make a difference: "As a student, and member of the basketball and volleyball teams, I had the opportunity to see Coach Selfe almost daily at the King Center. I also had the pleasure of having Professor Selfe for a few classes. After I graduated I continued to faithfully attend Homecoming. Passing through the King Center to play volleyball and visit with friends became an annual ritual I looked forward to with great anticipation. Except the year my mother died. She passed away in August and as the annual game rolled around in October I really couldn't get past my grief and depression. I decided, apprehensively, to go back to Emory thinking maybe getting away would be good and that seeing old friends might help with the pain. As usual, I headed into the gym and there was Coach Selfe standing in front of the coaches' offices talking to a recruit and his family. He immediately stopped talking with the visitors, walked over to me, put his arm around me and said, 'Hello Miss Williams. I am so sorry to hear about your mother passing away. You take care.' It never occurred to me to ask how he knew about my mom, and it really didn't matter because his words were spoken from his great big heart. He never knew how those words impacted me. Simple words from a man I respected. He made my decision to attend that Homecoming the beginning of my healing process . . . thanks to a wonderful man and his kind words."

Steve Allen says a small act by Fred Selfe was the deciding factor in his choice to attend Emory and Henry: "I was trying to choose between Emory, VMI and Murray State. I was so involved with track I couldn't find the time to drive back to Emory from Christiansburg. Coach Selfe showed up at my track meet in Wytheville, brought me to Emory and personally showed me around the campus. I was impressed by his willingness to go out his way for me. He took the time to drive the 50 or so miles to make sure I got another chance to see the campus. I made my decision then and there . . . Fred's willingness to help me made all the difference in my choice of colleges and that has made the difference in my life."

Use the lessons of how and why Fred Selfe lived his life to find ways you can make your own life better. Live a life of courage. Choose the character you wish to see in the mirror each morning. Take legendary coach Lou Holtz's advice: "Everybody is looking for instant success, but it doesn't work that way. You build a successful life one day at a time."

Share these lessons with others; do something for someone else. You can become the most *successful* person you know.

Beat your wings and drum up a storm.

THIRD
GREAT BIG
SMALL THING

Courageous and Contagious

Come to the edge,' he said.
They said, 'We are afraid.'
'Come to the edge,' he said.
They came.
He pushed them . . . And they flew.

Guillaume Apollinaire

Courage comes in two flavors: physical and moral. Physical courage is the strong, sweet flavor that inspired the image of our traditional epic heroes: young men slaying ferocious beasts in France's 20,000 year-old cave paintings; Israel's young David knocking over the giant Goliath with a single stone from his sling; Ireland's Cuchulainn destroying the enemies of Ulster; Macedon's young Alexander conquering Greece, Egypt, Babylon, Persia and the valley of the Indus; America's John Wayne fighting hostile Indians, bad hombres, and the soldiers of Imperial Japan, Nazi Germany and Communist North Vietnam during his long cinematic career.

Kings were chosen by the degree of it they possessed; monsters destroyed by a fist full of it, and empires conquered under its bright and shining banner. The men and women who possessed it grew to larger-than-life symbols of what we aspired to be; heroic.

Physical courage has become less needed in our modern world. We have few undiscovered Shangri-las to trek or wild expanses of uncharted land to survey; the monster Grendel and his mother no longer pillage our towns; most of the El Dorados and golden fleeces have been found, and few other than Ted Nugent go out to track and kill their dinner.

Perhaps it is why we flock to movies like the *Indiana Jones* and *The Lord of the Rings* series; good against evil, underdog against the mob, right against wrong. It seems even in these days of modern convenience, we still have a need for the rites of passage adventure and danger produce. Our dependency on that flavor drives us to marathon, climb Mount Everest, extreme kayak on the Yangtze River, pay to go into space in a Russian Soyuz rocket, or leave graduate school to bootstrap a high-risk business venture from our garage. We honor and crave the physical courage it takes to push our human limits.

Moral courage can be salty and bitter to taste. It is certainly not as easy to spot as the physical kind; perhaps because it is such a personal thing and the few people who show it actually care to make it public knowledge. According to Rush Kidder, president of the Institute for Global Ethics, moral courage is facing challenges that "could harm one's reputation, emotional well-being, self-esteem, or other characteristics." Mr. Kidder continues to explain moral courage encompasses the courage to be: honest, fair, respectful, responsible and compassionate, and that acts of moral courage carry "the risks of humiliation, ridicule, contempt, unemployment, and loss of social standing." Here is where moral courage differs from physical courage; instead of being rewarded for their actions, those who are successful in showing moral courage are usually punished for it.

Give some thought to those remembered for displaying extreme moral courage: Oskar Schindler, Martin Luther King Jr., Nelson Mandela, Mother Teresa, Mahatma Gandhi, Lech Walesa, Vaclav Havel, Aung San Suu Kyi. All chose to act when it was unpopular, dangerous and often life-threatening. Each reached the limit of their personal moral *logos*, principles, to take a stand against the rising tide of an injustice. None can say Martin Luther King Jr. did the convenient thing, or Gandhi chose the easy way. Moral courage is, by nature, the difficult path—Robert Frost's *road not taken*, and requires more real courage than the adrenaline-inspired strength of the physical.

In their book, *The Art of Possibility*, Rosamund Stone Zander and Benjamin Zander offer a story of King Christian X of Denmark shortly after the Nazi occupation of the Danish capital in 1940. King Christian looked out the window of the palace to find the red, black and white swastika flying over the roofs of the government buildings and immediately called for a meeting with the Nazi commander. The King requested the flag be removed. The Nazi officer refused. King Christian walked a few feet away, and spent some more moments in thought. He approached the officer once more.

The King asked, "And what will you do if I send a soldier to take it down?"

"I will have him shot," the officer replied.

"I don't believe you will," said the King quietly, "when you see the soldier I will send."

The officer demanded the sovereign explain himself.

"I will be the soldier," said King Christian.

The flag came down within the day.

The King could have done as other heads of states around him and gone into exile or simply capitulated to Hitler's advances and the rising tide of fascism. Instead, the King stayed in the capital throughout the war, stood up to the Nazis, and actually rode through the streets on horseback each morning without a bodyguard. He and his fellow countrymen helped thousands of Danish Jews when Hitler ordered their roundup. For his defiance, the Nazis forced him from the throne and broke up the Danish government in 1943.

Pat Tillman is a modern moral hero. Tillman was so moved by the terrorist attacks of September 11th he chose to leave a highly-lucrative career with the Arizona Cardinals football team to enlist in the U.S. Army and fight in Afghanistan. He exited the NFL without fanfare or even a press conference. He quietly walked away from the money and fame to do what he considered the "right thing." In April, 2004, Pat Tillman was killed in an ambush outside a small Afghan town wearing the uniform of the elite Army Rangers.

There are others, but it becomes exceedingly difficult to name a great number of people in our modern age one considers heroic. In fact, a Harris Interactive poll found more than half of all Americans could name *no public figure alive today they considered heroic*. To add salt to that wound, one-in-six said they *had no hero at all*.

Then again, maybe our perception of heroes is skewed. As Joseph Badaracco, Jr. points out in his work *A Lesson For The Time: Learning From Quiet Leaders*, "The problem . . . is that we spend too much time on the stories of men and women who have reshaped the world, led great political or moral crusades, or transformed companies or industries. Sometimes ostensibly small acts influence other people months or even years later—by taking root in their experience, gestating and shaping their development. And, even when larger consequences do not result from small acts, they simply matter because they are the right thing to do."

What Would Fred Selfe Do

In researching this book, I met people from all stages of Fred Selfe's life who see this simple coach and teacher as the very fount of their own moral courage. When faced with life's challenges thousands of men and women ask themselves *"What would Coach Selfe do?"* He is the crucible that shaped the lives of so many young men and women and the example by which they judge their rights and wrongs. He is the kind of real-life hero we need in this time without heroes.

It takes courage to stand your ground and show tough love. Fred Selfe was a man who showed tough love as part of his very character. "Your husband was truly a giant," writes Dr. Timothy McGarry to Becky Selfe, "not merely amongst football coaches, but as a truly loving and caring person. Coach Selfe was the embodiment of the term *tough love*. He pushed those kids on the football field, but he never pushed them in a negative way. He never once let a player cheat or go through the cracks because Coach Selfe knew what it took to get the most out of one's ability. Coach Selfe was tough, but his love for the kids came shining through at all turns."

Paul Overbay, a record-breaking receiver with 27 NCAA career touchdown receptions, played on the *Wasps* teams of 1985-88 and is now a teacher and football coach at Science Hill High School in his hometown of Johnson City, Tennessee. "I thought I knew what coaching was all about," Paul says, "until I became one. Every day is another challenge; teaching in a chaotic environment, the lack of discipline, kid's personal problems, trying to turn a bunch of young individuals into a cohesive team working together . . . it just goes on and on. Coaching and teaching are an unrelenting series of tough questions and a constant search for the right answers. These questions go to bed with me at night and wake up with me in the morning. I find myself, at least once a day, asking myself what Coach Selfe would do in this situation or that one. He was so respectful and genuine he commanded not only respect, but also everyone's best efforts. I always tried to give him my best. His face and voice immediately pop into my head and offer me guidance each time I need it— maybe because he taught and coached every chance he got with you. That's what lets me sleep at night."

Joe-Joe Collins, a receiver from Cleveland, Tennessee who played on the same teams says earning and retaining Coach Selfe's respect is what drove him to work harder to be better. Collins explains that Fred Selfe's courage to be different—to be strong and "upright"— made him a paragon and attracted people who wanted to believe in something greater. The mere thought of disappointing Coach Selfe made Collins feel "sick at his stomach" and "small." He experienced feelings of extreme dread when confronted with his failure to live up to the standards of the man he admired. Only when we respect someone do we care what they think of our actions, and only when we truly admire someone do we accept their standards as our own. Collin's need to retain the respect of Fred Selfe shows his elevation from coach to hero. Why do so many of us feel the same? Emory and Henry head men's basketball coach Bob Johnson, who has over 300 wins and five trips to the national championships, may have the answer to that question when he says, "[Fred Selfe] *is* Emory and Henry. He's the heart and soul of this place, and he influenced hundreds of students, both male and female. People . . . wanted to do the right thing wherever he was concerned because we didn't want to disappoint him."

He was not a wealthy man; there were no television shows to find an apprentice for him, or major philanthropic foundations that bear his name. He was not a socially or politically powerful man; no politicians called to seek his advice, nor would you have seen him at many cocktail parties. He did not drive an expensive car, or dress in expensive clothes. In fact, as his friend Bob Johnson ribs, "I've got to tell you—this guy—he was a wonderful man . . . but the guy was *not* a great dresser. Although I have to say he made quite a fashion statement out of blue shorts and gray t-shirts."

Fred Selfe's most evident trait—the one that makes him stand out from the crowd is his courage. From his childhood in Castlewood, Virginia in which the nerves of one eye were severed causing a lifelong disability of double vision, to the death of his father at age 11 years, to his own long fight with cancer, Fred Selfe showed simple personal courage inspiring those who knew him.

His physical strength is legend. Wayne Neese, a former *Wasp* teammate, said, "If he was blocking you he had you on your back . . . he'd kick your butt in a minute."

LeRoy Strohl, Director of Libraries for the University of Mary Washington in Fredericksburg, Virginia, was director of Emory and Henry's Kelly Library from 1974-1984 and a former neighbor of the Selfes. He attests to Fred Selfe's physical might: "For a number of years we lived on 'Rabbit Row' . . . The Selfes shared a driveway with us and our porches faced each other. My daughters Meg and Mary really liked their *Uncle Fred* because he always seemed to have time for them, and they always kept an eye open for whatever he was doing. Fred and Becky had a Volkswagen Beetle . . . Fred did his own maintenance and took pretty good care of that car. On a summer day [Cathy] and the children were sitting on the porch, when my oldest daughter looked over to see Fred working on the Beetle. Meg asked what Uncle Fred was doing. Cathy looked over to see that Fred, who was one of the strongest men I have ever met, wasn't actually working on the car; he was lifting the rear end of the car up by the bumper to shift it over just a little bit for some reason. Cathy simply replied, 'Meg, your Uncle Fred is moving his car,' as if it was an everyday feat."

He was an All-American lineman on an offense that set a national record of more than 550 yards per game; he lifted pianos, and did the work of three men at summer construction. However it was his inner strength—his ability to stick to his own set of guiding principles through thick and thin—that drew people to him. His moral courage was manifest by living the principles he espoused; actually being the man others thought him to be.

In an editorial in a 2003 *Emory and Henry Alumni* magazine, Bob Johnson describes his friend and coaching colleague Fred Selfe as an ideal leader with a distinctive character: "His capacity to give was unique, well beyond what could be even unreasonably expected of anyone. I labeled him a *Foxhole Christian*. I believed then, and I still do, that at some point in his life he, or someone close to him, was in some horrible, life-threatening situation and Fred made a personal deal with God: 'God if you get me out of this, I'll live the life you want me to live.' Fred kept his word."

Fred Selfe's courage to live his principles should make us all pause to realize how few people do that in our world today. Instead of being a strong, principled and courageous society we are often the opposite—so few of us are morally courageous. It is like the story of the swayback nag and the city fellow who drove his car into the ditch near Emory a few years ago.

A stranger to the mountains of Southwestern Virginia was driving down a country road near Emory. Driving along enjoying the natural beauty of the area, he loses control of his car and winds up stuck in the ditch. A local farmer comes along with an old swayback horse pulling a hay wagon and offers to help the stranger.

The farmer hooks the old horse up to the car and walks up in front of the horse and calls out, "Pull *Buck*!"

Nothing happens. He waits a few seconds and calls out again, "Pull *Clyde*!"

Another few seconds go by and the old horse just sits there. The farmer gets closer and puts his hand on the horse's neck and yells, "Pull *Dusty*!"

The horse gives a mighty pull and the car pops out of the ditch and back onto the road.

The driver enthusiastically shakes the farmer's hand and thanks him, but says he is puzzled by something, "Why did you call out three different horse's names when you only have the one horse"

The farmer replies, "Well, Dusty there used to be my best horse, but he's old and almost blind. Dusty gets pretty discouraged if he thinks he is the only one doing the work."

Too many of us are like the old horse, we do not show courage unless we know others are doing it too. We read polls to see which way the winds of convenience and popularity are blowing then *go with the flow*. We sit on the fence until it is safe to be courageous and there is little risk. We are like the two Russians at the rear of a very long line. After about half an hour, one says to the other, "*What are we in line for*?" The other turns and replies, "*I have no idea but the line is long so it must be good.*"

Many are willing to blindly follow; few open their eyes and lead.

Saddle Up

Fred Selfe did not use a weather vane to see which way the winds of right or wrong were blowing. He did what he thought to be right every day of his life because it was part of who he was. It was the greatest part of his character to be a good person, serve others and help ease their burdens, teach others to teach, grow and shape young lives, work hard at the tasks he chose, provide for and protect those he loved, learn, be honest, live simply, be strong, and persevere. Few of those around him met the same standards, so there was no wagon onto which he could jump—not that he would have even if there had been one. He drove his own wagon; built it with his own hands, and others jumped on because they liked where he was going.

"When my generation of E&H athletes thinks of a role model or positive influence from our years at Emory, it will always be Coach Selfe," says Bill Mercer a 1976 Emory and Henry graduate. "We are so fortunate that there are so many people over his 27 years that can and do say the same thing."

I am one of those people.

I do not know anyone as principled as Coach Fred Selfe. In fact, I believe the paradox created by my early respect of heroes and the real lack of strong, courageous people in the world is shared by many others. It is why finding someone like Fred Selfe is such an anomaly—why he stands out as worthy of a book of principles and lessons.

Like every other human, I have faced—and continue to face—challenges and adversities. I have seen the limp dead body of a stranger killed by a drunken driver, hard working people figuratively robbed and beaten by business associates, alcoholics destroy themselves and those who love them, hunger in the face of a child, loneliness on the hands of the old holding on for one more moment; the pain, suffering and hopelessness of our human condition. I weep for it. My sensitivity and empathy keep it all with me like vivid snapshots; negatives burnt onto the back of my eyelids when I close them to escape it all. I remember every detail down to the color of the clothing and make of shoes on the lifeless stranger I helped pull from the small, mangled truck on Christmas Day many years ago. I cannot forget it no matter how hard I try.

Dr. Priya Patil is an epidemiologist and a good friend working to help treat and stop the rampant spread of HIV in Africa. She travels to Kenya, Nigeria, Uganda, Rwanda, and South Africa each month and upon her return recounts so many stories of abject human suffering I have no idea how she gets out of bed in the morning: Babies dying in their mother's arms, young men wasting away in front of their families, old women dropping dead of hunger in the slums of Nairobi or Kampala or Kigali.

When I am overwhelmed by the grief and suffering of the world and seek understanding, I turn to my own religious faith and Fred Selfe's lesson of one good, courageous person making a difference. I am reminded each of us can do something—a small thing—to make it better.

As I mentioned in the *First Great Big Small Thing*, over three million people are directly and indirectly influenced by Fred Selfe's courage to live his life each day by a guiding set of traditional principles. Toni O'Neil, in a personal note to the Selfe family writes, "He was an exceptional person in so many ways . . . a gentle giant of a man with such wonderful intellect, kindness, dignity and extraordinary courage."

Three million people and counting! If we use Fred Selfe's *butterfly effect* to shape our own lives—become like him, we make it exponential. Our little wings will beat and drum up a huge storm of new, better, more courageous servant leaders for our culture . . . and that can make all the difference in the world.

To begin to create in ourselves the kind of courage Fred Selfe showed, we must first come to grips with our fears and accept as fact we do not currently possess enough courage. Perhaps you have fears and challenges as a father or mother, in your business, or in your community. It could be in a relationship, or as a teacher or coach. Wherever the wrong is occurring, wherever courage is needed you can do what need be done to make it better. As British political philosopher, Edmund Burke, warned, "All that is necessary for the triumph of evil is that good men do *nothing*."

If you are a Christian, you know Jesus rebuked the church at Laodicea. Jesus had an angel write letters to His seven churches around the world, most of which are kind and helpful, sometimes warning them against their actions, but, for the most part positive. To Laodicea, however, He had nothing good to say. Laodicea was a prosperous manufacturing city in Asia known for its fine, glossy black wool and a popular healing eye salve made from alum. It was also the banking center for the whole of Asia Minor—modern Turkey. The people of the city smugly considered themselves rich, however; Jesus pronounces them poor in spirit. In a letter to the church at Laodicea in the Book of Revelations 3:14, He says: "I know thy works, that thou *art neither cold nor hot. I would thou were cold or hot.* So then because thou art lukewarm, and neither cold nor hot, I will spew thee out of My mouth." He told them in the letter they make him vomit and chastises them for having everything but doing nothing. The people were lukewarm, halfhearted, and apathetic—they sat on the fence. Jesus' warning is a clear one; warm up. In fact, get hot and get about doing the things you fear doing. Fear is the decision not to be courageous—turn the table and make a stand.

We all have fears. I have a fear of heights. When I look down from a high point, I experience the physical effects of light-headedness and loss of balance. No matter how many times I tell myself I am not acrophobic, when I get to a great height and look down the same weakening effects occur. I tried for many years to deny I had the fear. I would get out on the roof of a skyscraper or a scenic overlook while hiking, look over the edge and get the old familiar feelings of dizziness and cold sweats.

I finally accepted my fear and set about getting into a position where the fear would occur so I could learn to deal with it. I asked my friend Tim Sams to teach me to rock climb and repel. Having grown up on the side of a mountain in the wilds of Cedar Bluff, Virginia climbing a rock wall was no big feat; repelling— lowering oneself over a 150 foot cliff held only by a thin rope laced through a waist harness scared the daylights out of me.

The first step—the one that places the climber at a perpendicular angle to the rock so gravity can take over and draw the climber down was a waking nightmare. I stood on the very edge of the cliff high up on the Skyline Drive near Stanardsville, Virginia, for more than 15 minutes—which seemed more like an hour and 15 minutes; frozen in one spot. I could not move. Tim could sense my reluctance and, with great patience, worked to help me lean back an inch at a time until I could take the first great step that would mean no return. After that first step the world beneath me changed. Suddenly the fear was under control. I repelled to the bottom of the cliff and hurried back up to do it again. The second time was less difficult than the first, but the fear was still there—only controlled that time. The third time that day was much like the second; I now understood the rope and harness would hold me and what I could expect from the descent. The fear was still there but under my control—control that comes from understanding what was once unknown.

Real courage is come by in an honest way: Learn to control the fear and the courage to do the right thing becomes easier each time you try it. John Wayne, America's embodiment of grit and determination said, "Courage is being scared to death and saddling up anyway."

Bronwyn Reynolds, a 1980-84 E&H women's basketball player, tells a story that wonderfully describes Fred Selfe's willingness to *saddle up* and the strong influence his courage had on those who knew him: "One Friday night we were to play our biggest rival–Roanoke College. We lived for that game! The game with Roanoke went as usual—it was close and very physical. Every second was crucial. I remember diving for a loose ball to save it from going out of bounds and slid right into Coach Selfe. He saved me from hitting my head on his chair, picked me up like a wet rag, looked me in the eye and said, "Good hustle, Munchkin! *Get back out there*!" His eyes were stern and motivated, and with that, so was I. We won that game. Last year at a home women's basketball game I found out Coach Selfe was in the hospital fighting for his life. I felt scared because I knew I had to go and see him the next morning. I hesitated fearing I would see him weak and frail, but I walked in to find him sitting on the edge of his hospital bed, talking to his brother. Although he had an oxygen tube attached he was still the same strong, determined coach and teacher I remembered. I wanted so badly to run over there and hug him. He must have sensed that because he smiled and said, "I would hug you Munchkin, but they won't allow me to." I just nodded my head so he knew that I understood, but what he didn't know was that he did hug me, just then, with his kind eyes and his words. We caught up with each other and in all that time he never mentioned cancer, or how he was feeling and I never asked. This was the great man I knew who never said a curse word or a negative word about anything or anyone, and never showed any emotional downs since the day I met him. He wasn't about to do it then. As I was departing I turned, looked at him and as I welled up inside I told him, "You know, you were always my dad away from home, and you still are." He looked down at his feet, nodded his head and with great respect and care softly said, "I know . . . and I appreciate that." I looked at him, and remembering that basketball game many years before I told him, "You fight, and *get back in there*." He responded, just as I knew he would, "I am going to beat this."

Fred Selfe emitted strength and courage the way a strong battery gives off a current. You could sense it—feel it—when you were close to him. Courage was his core.

There are five factors—*small things*—that contribute to courage; things you will want to work on individually to shore-up the bigger thing:

1)   Purpose

Have one. Look inside and know what it is you need to face head on. Say it aloud—shout it to the world and notice how good it feels to accept it. You may want to write it down and tape it up on the mirror into which you gaze each morning—a place where it will announce and affirm itself each day. Whatever you need to do to own it, do it.

2)   Candor

Speak up and speak out. Tell it like it is. Tell the truth about *it* whatever *it* may be. Be tactful and respectful of others, but whatever you do—tell the truth. It is an act of courage to say things others will not. When you do you will find you respect yourself for doing it—and others will respect you too.

3)   Resolve

Maintain it. Keep it up. Each morning when you take a long look at your purpose, vow to work on it *that* very day. Do that until it becomes unnecessary to *make* yourself do it—it becomes what you do automatically. Resolve is your inner strength and a necessity for courage to make an appearance.

4)   **Risk**

Accept it. Life is one risk followed by another. There is a possibility your courage will not carry the day, but, when you avoid risk you simply put off an opportunity to even fight the battle. If you run from risk you accept mediocrity—you accept what you are given instead of going after what you want on your own terms.

5)   **Role Models**

Find one. Most of us do not know *the way*, so we search for people who do. We then have to follow them—emulate and imitate their actions until they become our actions. Find good role models, like Fred Selfe, and become that person.

THREE GREAT BIG SMALL THINGS

1)   *As Iron Sharpens Iron*, Your Life Can Sharpen So Many Others
2)   Beat Your Wings
3)   Be Courageous and Contagious

The *Third Great Big Small Thing* of the *Selfe Factor* is to make courage the center of your life—your core. Do what needs be done—if it is the right thing—do it regardless of what others may think or what consequences may come. Take John Wayne's advice, *saddle up* and refuse to allow fear of the unknown stop you. When you live this kind of courageous life, choose a side in an issue, jump off the fence, do the right thing even though it is unpopular, stand up to the status quo when it is wrong, you can expect to attract lightening like a metal rod in a summer storm. *Money* magazine reports Charles Munger, vice chairman of Berkshire Hathaway and contemporary of Warren Buffet, added to Buffet's advice at the 2004 investors meeting to spend time with people who are better than you: "If this gives you a little temporary unpopularity with your peer group the hell with 'em."

That is usually the reward for moral courage. Supreme Court Justice Clarence Thomas, certainly no stranger to controversy, says he is not surprised more good people do not get involved in civic life "when one observes the pitched battles that rage around persons of strong convictions." However, Justice Thomas adds, "I do believe we are required to wade into those things that matter to our country and culture, no matter the disincentive, and no matter the personal cost."

On the other side of the coin, you may also expect to receive the same kind of respect Fred Selfe is afforded. Persons who respect themselves and are strong among the weak become icons. They are the people we want to be—heroes.

When you make the decision to be courageous you may experience what Carl Jung called *synchronicity*—meaningful and inexplicable coincidences. For instance, you spend many agonizing months deciding which brand of new car to purchase and finally settle on the Chevrolet

Suburban. Suddenly, everywhere you turn you see Chevy Suburbans. That is synchronicity.

Once you decide to accept courage and begin to act with it, you will see it everywhere. You will be drawn to others who display courage and it will bolster your own actions. With apologies to Jung, it may not be quite as inexplicable as he theorized, but the simple cause and effect of being a courageous person. Your courage will grow exponentially until you find yourself in direct opposition to the injustices and unfairness that exists in our world.

Your courage will draw you into a community of other courageous people—and those communities will change the world one neighborhood at a time.

Learn from Fred Selfe's life to become courageous and contagious.

FOURTH
GREAT BIG
SMALL THING

Structural Integrity

Your life may be the only Bible some people read.

Anonymous

In the early 1960s my father dropped out of college and went home to live with my grandparents. He was flat broke and depressed; the world looked hopeless.

The first day he was home, my grandfather came in and told him that his business partners had gotten so excited when they heard my father was back in town they asked if he might like to come to work with them. My father was surprised and flattered by the offer. He cheered up a bit and told my grandfather he'd like to go to work at the small coal-mining company. He worked there for six months or so, made some money, regained his self-esteem and went back to college. It is a sweet family story we passed around for years, but, like most oral history, hardly the whole story.

My grandfather, Benjamin F. McGlothlin II, passed away in 1975. A few years ago my father ran into one the original partners of the old Seaboard mine who told him what really occurred. It seems my grandfather gathered his partners and asked if his son might have a job at the small mine until he could get himself back up on his feet. The partners, though they liked my father, said they really could not afford to hire him. My grandfather cut a deal with them: if they would hire my father, give him a paycheck every two weeks and keep it quiet, he would let them take the money out of his own meager paycheck. He knew what my father needed was a little bit of hope. So, he did it and never said a word about it. He did not hold it over my father or make him feel indebted in any way. He did it for no personal gain other than his son might grow strong from it and become happy.

This short story is one of the few things I have left of my grandfather. It keeps his memory alive and is one of the stories that make me admire and respect him. Every time I tell that story my grandfather's character shines brightly through all those years since I last saw him. It will continue to shine as I pass the story along to my children and they pass it along to theirs.

Someone described character as *what you are when no one is watching*. Another oft-quoted anonymous voice says your character is *what you are in the dark*. In other words your character is the real you. Like the selfless example of Benjamin F. McGlothlin II, character is what precedes you and what remains of your life after you are gone.

Better By Design

Integrity and virtues are the main ingredients of character. They are the elements that, when blended together, form the *roux* of our personal existence.

The first ingredient, integrity, is how well you are put together. It is your structure and composition. When we speak of the *integrity* of a building, we are discussing its soundness, completeness and wholeness—how well what is inside is put together. The building's structural integrity is its ability to withstand internal and external pressures. Our integrity is what gives us the ability to outlast the storms of life.

In information technology terms *integrity* means the degree to which data, or a database, has remained free from corruption or change; how true it remains to its original purity. Our integrity is the same. It is our inner strength that keeps us from being corrupted. We develop integrity over time through our experiences and observations of others, and we may increase our degree of integrity whenever we choose.

Douglas Bader lost both legs in a flying accident in England in 1931. He fought his way back to walk, drive a car, and, despite the protestations of most of his RAF superiors, fly again. He was so successful he became a flight commander of Spitfires and, with his new legs of worked tin, fought the Luftwaffe in the skies over Europe. Following a mid-air collision with a Messerschmitt, Bader was captured; his prosthetic legs destroyed in the crash. He escaped from the stalags so often the Germans finally remanded him to their most notorious *sonderlager*—high security prison; the infamous Colditz Castle. His courage earned even the Nazi's respect and they allowed a special British late night airdrop; the single package—a pair of new legs. It simply was not in Douglas "Tin Legs" Bader's character to surrender to anything: the loss of his legs, his RAF superiors, the Luftwaffe, or Nazis prisons. His integrity impressed even the enemy he was sworn to kill and defeat.

Virtues are the essence of our individual spirit and the content of our character; the individual qualities that make our character.

Our modern ideal of the virtues one should possess, the qualities we expect to find in *good character,* are derived from differing sources. Christian virtues, thanks to Paul, are defined simply as: faith, hope, and charity.

The key virtues of Buddhism are: *maitri* (friendliness, good-will, benevolence, love, kindness); *karuna* (compassion for the sufferings of all); *mudita* (joy in the good of all); *upeksha* (forgiveness, overlooking the faults of all.)

In classical philosophy, the four principle virtues are justice, prudence, fortitude, and temperance.

The seven cardinal virtues of medieval literature are: faith, hope, charity, prudence, temperance, chastity, and fortitude.

Ancient Rome had a laundry list of virtues to which every citizen was to aspire: *Dignitas* (dignity), *firmitas* (tenacity), *gravitas* (gravity), *humanitas* (humanity), *honestas* (honesty), *industria* (industriousness), *pietas* (dutifulness), *prudential* (prudence), *salubritas* (wholesomeness), *serveritas* (sternness), *veritas* (truthfulness), *frugalitas* (frugalness), *auctoritas* (spiritual authority), *comitas* (humor), *clementia* (mercy).

Regardless of which list we choose, our virtues are the best of our behavior and the ideals for which we strive. Perhaps it is why there was a clarion call over the hurly-burly of the mid-Clinton era: "*Character counts!*" When the character of our culture is running on empty, we find we need it most. Like the old saying, *you never miss your water until the well runs dry.*

We especially regard the character of our leaders to be sacrosanct. It is why the first strike in any political fight is usually *character assassination*; an attack intended to ruin someone's reputation. We Americans want, expect even, the character of our leaders to be above reproach. We are shocked when we learn a minister, teacher, or government official shows an un*characteristic* trait: theft, spousal abuse, drug addiction, lies, and anger. Our disappointment proves we have an ingrained expectation of what actually makes for good character.

George Washington "could not tell a lie."

Abraham Lincoln is remembered as "honest Abe."

George Washington Carver, as an infant in 1864, was kidnapped with his mother by Confederate night-raiders. His mother was never found. Carver went on to develop 325 products from peanuts, over 200 products from other vegetables, more than 118 industrial products, a rubber substitute, and over 500 dyes and pigments.

Helen Keller overcame blindness and illiteracy to become a world famous author, lecturer and champion of minorities and the underprivileged.

Brigadier General Anthony McAuliffe responded to German General Heinrich von Luttwitz's demand for the U.S. 101st Airborne *Screaming Eagle's* immediate surrender at Bastogne with a single word of defiance, "*Nuts!*"

Cal Ripken Jr. played through pain and sickness in a record-breaking 2,216 consecutive games.

Lance Armstrong was given a 40 percent chance of recovery from cancer, yet fought back, survived the cancer and continues to dominate the Tour de France.

We want to follow people who exemplify the things we want to be.

A Man of Virtue

Fred Selfe is known for his stainless steel character. Almost all of those I interviewed talked about his "strong character" or go on about how he was a "man of great integrity." Most, like me, say he possessed the highest degree of character of anyone they know. He was constantly teaching others how to do the right thing through his example. Paul Overbay remembers his character did not require words to be powerful: "One year at Homecoming, the end-zone crowd of E&H fans was giving the refs and other players a difficult time to the point of coming onto the field beyond the 'yellow rope.' The ref came over to Coach Selfe and told him a penalty was on the way if they did not stop. Coach Selfe started walking toward the end-zone, but as he got closer the entire crowd of 200 people froze, then stepped back five or so yards and stayed there for the entire game."

His integrity was as large as the "gentle colossus" himself. He stood toe-to-toe with many of life's greatest challenges: the early loss of a parent, raising a child while in college, playing All-American caliber football with double vision in one eye, cancer—he stared them all down. Took them on with stolid pride and clinched fists. He was as solid as the rock that now sits in the far corner of the end zone at Emory and Henry's football field, bearing a plaque in his honor to be touched by each player as they come onto the field to do battle. The plaque is engraved with some simple advice Coach Selfe often gave his players: *Trust in your teammates. Trust in yourself.*

"Coach Selfe was a man of strong, yet compassionate character," says Bronwyn Reynolds, "When I first met him I could feel his mental and emotional strength, his passion for athletics, his love for education, but mostly, he showed me right from the beginning, his ability to teach. And I don't mean just classroom teaching, but teaching by actions, by his words, and just by his mere presence. He was a big and strong man physically, but in my eyes and my heart he was even bigger."

The virtues that made up his character are taken straight from those classic virtues I listed above: He *walked his talk* each day; he genuinely cared about those with whom he came in contact; he knew your name and most likely your jersey number if you ever played football; he worked hard; he never complained; he was honest; he constantly worked for excellence and was unbending in that quest; he was humble and expected the same of his players— in four years I saw only one player *hotdog*, or showoff, and that was the biggest mistake that young man ever made. The *Wasp* receiver made an amazing catch in the corner of the end zone through two defenders and got so excited he spiked the ball. In college football that is a 15-yard penalty; at Emory it is worse. Coach Selfe immediately pulled him out of the game and did not put him back in—*and he was a starting receiver*! For Coach Selfe, the game of football was about the team—never the individual. Playing was like a job, you do it the best you can and go home.

He was more impressed by doing things well than by winning. Don't get me wrong, he loved to win, but, to him winning is an outcome of doing things "the best you can do." Phillip Henley remembers an unscripted move that got him in hot water with Coach Selfe in a game in 1981 against Division II powerhouse Hampton Institute—now *Division I powerhouse* Hampton University: "We were trying to score when—as I was being tackled—I had the bright idea to lateral the ball to one of my teammates. We actually got a few yards on the play, but that did not matter to Coach Selfe. He called a timeout and personally called me to the sidelines. I went there like a humbled dog with *my tail tucked between my legs*. After a tirade of '*Gosh dandies*' and '*Bullfrogs*,' his final words to me as I left for the huddle were, 'Henley, if you don't score on this play it's a long walk back to Emory.' Needless to say,"

Henley adds with a smile, "I scored a touchdown because I was afraid not to score."

He gave praise easily, but refused it when it came his way. He never took the credit for any victory, but always shouldered blame for defeat. He was strong. He helped others. He was not impressed by power, titles or money—he was impressed by those who exemplified the same virtues he possessed. In fact his yardsticks for measuring others were character, hard work and humility. He told his wife Becky the person he most admired was Fred Holbrook—a man with whom he worked on summer construction—a quiet man who possessed great skill with his hands and worked hard.

The *Fourth Great Big Small Thing* you can learn from Fred Selfe's life is to work to be a person of great character. Shore up your integrity; make yourself a well-built house capable of weathering any storm. Choose the virtues you deem important for good living and make them part of what you do each day.

Fred Selfe cared about his integrity and the character of those around him. Becky Selfe, Coach Selfe's partner and "bride" of 38 years, recounts their first date as anything but ordinary: "He was 15 and I was 14 at the time. He asked me, '*What are your principles*?' I had no idea what he was talking about . . . *who* are my principals . . . you mean at school? I felt silly. Principles, what people are made of, were important to him even at that age."

Nancy Hockett Howlett grew up in the town of Emory and attended Emory and Henry. She thought about other schools, but soon decided on the neighboring college. "My senior year of high school we started looking at colleges. Emory was of no interest to me since I grew up just across the railroad tracks from campus. While being shown around Carson Newman College in Jefferson City, Tennessee we were surprised to run into Fred Selfe standing in the middle of the road. The E&H baseball team was there playing a game. Coach Selfe stopped, looked at us and said, 'You're NOT actually considering this are you, Miss Hockett?' in that deliberate tone we all know was more of a command than a question. My mother and I thanked the folks at Carson Newman, got into our car and drove back to Emory—decision made."

Nancy's understanding of the subtle message was bolstered by the receipt of a graduation gift from the Selfes; a pair of athletic sweats emblazoned with the Emory and Henry logo.

Nancy's father, Leo Hockett, was one of the football teams' biggest fans, often pulling his yellow pick-up truck in the shade of the locust trees that border the field to watch practices and showing up at away games long before the team got there. He and Fred Selfe worked summers building houses and were good friends. Nancy tells a story of Fred Selfe's strength of character and how it made him do for others. "Dad came up with plans to build a playground for my young son, Devin, but, unfortunately, his health declined before he could build it. The following spring, Coach Selfe came to me and told me Dad had explained the whole plan and they'd been ready to build it, but time didn't allow before Dad died. Later on that summer Fred just showed up one day at our house near Roanoke. He and Becky pulled up all smiles with a trailer loaded down with building materials. Fred pulled it all off the trailer and began the long process of setting it up in the yard. When he finished, he included a little something extra—a wooden plaque with my son's name engraved on it. A few weeks later, he and Becky dropped in again. He'd decided there was a better place in the yard to set the playground and driven all that way just to move it. Fred Selfe collected the material, built the playground and came back to position it correctly because of an unspoken duty to my Dad."

Nathan Graybeal, the college's Sports Information Director reinforces that sentiment, "Selfe was a man of utmost integrity and honor . . . a lot of things he did most people didn't see. If there was a big snow he'd go to [sick and elderly people's] houses and clear their driveways. Sometimes they wouldn't even know who did it. That's the kind of man he was."

Mike Griffith played with Fred Selfe on the successful *Wasp* teams of the late 1960s. Although he started his football career at the Virginia Military Institute, Griffith moved to Emory and Henry and found himself smack-dab in the middle of a "high-powered offense;" one that often ran over 100 plays in a single game. Though nervous about joining an already established offensive line, he was welcomed, and immediate befriended by "the leader of that gang."

Soon enough he was roped into going with that leader, Fred Selfe, to the college president's office to discuss the low pay football coaches were receiving. For two young players to walk the long walk to the president's office then sit across a desk from the most powerful man on the campus is a pretty daunting experience—one Fred Selfe took upon himself because he believed it needed doing. Sitting in front of the school's president, surrounded by antique mahogany furniture, award plaques and all the trappings of office did not scare him. He was doing the right thing.

Griffith relates how he sat quietly as Fred Selfe laid out their case for increasing the coaches' pay with the skill of a trained attorney addressing a courtroom. "President Finch was not receptive, says Griffith, "but Fred made one hell of a case. I was impressed with his intelligence and his ability to look you dead in the face and articulate what was on his mind." The argument, however, did not convince President Finch to increase the pay for the football coaches and soon cost the college its head football coach, Casto Ramsey, who accepted a higher paid assistant coaching position with Virginia Tech.

Oddly enough, Fred Selfe met Coach Ramsey on a Virginia high school all-star team for which Selfe was chosen to play. Ramsey was the head coach of the Virginia team in a post-season game against neighboring West Virginia. Ramsey immediately saw the potential of the young, smart, naturally strong and fast boy from Castlewood. Though Fred Selfe entered Virginia Tech his first year, Ramsey continued to pursue him and eventually convinced him to come and play at Emory. Casto Ramsey built a powerhouse football team over the next four years with Selfe commanding the record-setting offensive line. Selfe was awarded All-American honors his senior year on the 1968 nine wins, one loss team and Ramsey left for Blacksburg. Griffith says, "Man, did I miss Coach Ramsey the following season, but I think I missed Fred more."

FOUR GREAT BIG SMALL THINGS

1)   *As Iron Sharpens Iron,* Your Life Can Sharpen So Many Others
2)   Beat Your Wings
3)   Be Courageous and Contagious
4)   Build a Strong House

I decided my senior year to turn my bandana into a political statement. I wore a bright yellow bandana under my helmet to catch the sweat and ease the discomfort of the helmet's liner. One afternoon, after watching a television documentary in my dorm room, I decided to add a message to the bandana with a black marker. In the game on Saturday I was standing on the sidelines with my helmet off waiting to go in for my set of plays, when a hand jerked my shoulder pads back and around. After I stopped spinning I found myself face to face with Coach Selfe. He looked over his dark glasses with his head cocked to the side and read the words "Stop Apartheid" on my bandana. He was silent for about three seconds then asked, "That statement means something to you?" I sheepishly responded, "Yes, sir. I think South Africa should stop oppressing people of color." He shook his head in understanding and replied, "Me too, but right now get out there and run *34 Ram*," and pushed me onto the field. He understood my bandana message was a small act of courage—a small part of my character—he certainly would not stop me acting on my beliefs.

Learn the third of Fred Selfe's life lessons well. Once you read this book, you can ask yourself what Fred Selfe would do, see how he did it and do it yourself. Do the right thing each and every day—not for recognition or reward, but simply because it needs be done. Work on building your character. It is the foundation on which your personal *house* is built. Choose your virtues and place them stone by stone until you are strong and who you wish to be. Remember though, while you may be physically strong, it is your strength of character that gives you true integrity. In 1530 the Knights of St. John—more commonly known as the Knights of Malta—were headquartered in an impregnable fortress called Valetta on the island of Malta. Valetta was such a massive stronghold it withheld a five month siege in 1565 by Ottoman Turks before the Turks gave up and withdrew in disgrace. Over the years that followed, however, the members of the Order became soft and reclusive. They stopped recruiting younger knights, ate, drank and enjoyed their fame and fortune. In the 1700s Napoleon Bonaparte took the "impregnable fortress" in less than a day. Napoleon explained, "The place certainly possessed immense physical means of resistance, but no moral strength whatsoever."

Build yourself into a house of unquestionable structural integrity.

FIFTH
GREAT BIG
SMALL THING

The Action Hero

Not the cry, but the flight of the wild duck,
leads the flock to fly and follow.

Chinese Proverb

Be the change you want to see in the world.

Mahatma Gandhi

The Quakers, early American radical Christians, are known today for their pacifism and championing of the abolitionist movement. George Fox, founder of the Quaker group *Society of Friends*, preached against slavery as early as the late 1600's. By 1696, the Quakers made their first official declaration of abolitionism in

Pennsylvania, in which they declared they would discourage the importation of slaves. This, however, did not convince all Quakers to give up the practice.

In 1743 John Woolman was a simple Quaker in New Jersey. At age 23, he was asked by an employer to write a bill of sale for a slave. Woolman was so bothered by this event he began speaking out against it. He soon realized to spread this important doctrine he would have to travel away from the comforts of his little valley and visit Quakers and bodies of Quakers in their own environs. So, he did just that. The slight Quaker traveled throughout the colonies for most of his life quietly talking to fellow Quakers about abolishing the un-Christian practice of slavery. His actions all but ended the use of slaves among Quakers and branded their sect a driving force in the American abolitionist movement. John Woolman put his principles into action and put his feet on the road. He *walked his talk.*

I had a client a few years ago who came to me for help making her small business "more productive." The business was stalled. She was losing revenue, spending more to get new customers, and losing some clients she had had for years. I agreed to spend a week with her observing how she processed work orders, interacted with subcontractors and analyzing the work flow of her organization. After the second day, I asked her to show me her home. We drove there in her car. She gave me the grand tour of the nice three bedroom house she shared with two small dogs. She talked about her work processes, the subcontractors she used and how they interacted. I had other concerns. The next day I pulled her aside and asked if we could meet and I took her out of the office to a nearby coffee shop to give my findings.

My short report over a café latte was simply this—*she was completely disorganized and that was negatively affecting her business.* Her reply was, *"What? But, I try to be organized. I work on it all the time."*

I pointed out her car was a mess; paper everywhere, trash in the seats and floors, files strewn all over the floorboard. In her bedroom the bed was unmade, clothes were all over the floor; dust covered the furniture. In her downstairs guest bathroom someone had started pulling off wallpaper to paint, but quit about a third of the way through. They had also tried a few paint colors on the patches of bare drywall, but left it unfinished. There was an empty cardboard tube where the toilet paper should be.

She began protesting that she may be "a bit disorganized" in her personal life, but when it came to business she was very organized. I showed her a series of digital photos of her office; customer files stacked everywhere with no system or reason for their placement, cups, plates and discarded fast food wrappers covered the desks, disks and CDs haphazardly dropped here and there. I then repeated a list of missed deadlines from her last four projects and pointed out she was late for our last three meetings and canceled two more the mornings of.

My recommendations were simple: First, she must accept she is a disorganized person. Secondly, she must stop *thinking and talking* about being organized and *organize*! If my client wanted to make her business more productive, more efficient and effective, she needed to *act* on her thoughts.

Actions Speak Louder

The point of my story is this, walking your talk is the difference between *wanting* and *having*. It is the difference between *thinking about* something and *being* that thing. To quote an Elvis Presley hit, "*A little less conversation/a little more action please!*"

To be a good person and do good for others you must, as John Woolman did, *walk your talk*. Not putting your desire into action is like getting out of bed, showering and shaving, putting on clothes, grabbing your briefcase and standing with your hand on the front doorknob without opening the door. You *want* to go to work. You have *made plans* to go to work. You have done all you need do to *go* to work. But, you will never *get* to work unless you open the door. That is the first action you must take. Then you must get in your car and start it. Next you must drive to your office, get out of the car, enter your office building, ride the elevator to your floor, go into your office and sit at your desk. Now you are *at* work. Action is the difference between wanting and getting. Like the work analogy, it is often a chain of small actions that results in getting what you want, where or who you want to be.

On February 1, 1960 four young black North Carolina Agricultural and Technical College freshmen, Ezell Blair Jr., David Richmond, Joseph McNeil, and Franklin McCain entered the Elm Street Woolworth's in downtown Greensboro to purchase school supplies and "sundry" items. They wandered over to the lunch counter to order coffee, but were refused service. The four young men quietly sat down at the "whites only" lunch counter. They were still sitting there when the store closed.

The next day a larger group of NCA&T students showed up at the lunch counter. Again the students were refused service and all sat peacefully until the store closed. An even larger group showed up the next day. On the fourth day, three white female students from a neighboring school joined. By day five, more than 300 demonstrators conducted a *sit-in*, as the event became known, at the Woolworth's department store.

The City of Greensboro came down hard on the protests arresting 45 of the students for trespassing. This only served to fuel the movement as students launched massive boycotts of segregated lunch counters across the city. Sales all over town fell sharply and storeowners became alarmed.

News of the peaceful protests and subsequent arrests spread quickly. In two short months the *sit-in movement* spread to 54 cities in nine states.

Six months after the four freshmen were first refused service they returned to Woolworth's and were served lunch. Their simple and peaceful sit-ins ended restaurant and lunch-counter segregation in 26 southern cities and made a great stride in the movement toward Civil Rights.

These young men could have walked away when they were first refused. They could have just accepted the inevitable refusal and walked away. Instead they bravely sat at a whites-only lunch counter and waited amid people who did not want them there; people with a stake in protecting the status quo. The students gathered their principles and put them into action—in this case, sitting down instead of standing up for the right thing. Leaving the lunch counter and talking about what they *should have done* would have had no effect, whatsoever, on the American Civil Rights movement. Acting on their principles made all the difference in our country's current proud degree of equality.

To be courageous you must show courage. To be a person of good character you must use the virtues that make up that character each and every day. It is very much as former President Jimmy Carter says of his own choice, "I have one life and one chance to make it count for something—I'm free to choose what that something is, and the something I've chosen is my faith. Now, my faith goes beyond theology and religion and requires considerable work and effort. My faith demands—this is not optional—my faith demands that I do whatever I can, wherever I am, whenever I can, for as long as I can with whatever I have to try to make a difference."

This *want* versus *have* concept is represented by many terms: *walk your talk, proof is in the pudding, actions speak louder than words, practice what you preach.* All, however, describe the disparity marketing professionals refer to as the *want-got gap*—the thing(s) that keep you from possessing what you want. Lack of action is the gap. Dreaming, wanting, wishing, thinking and talking about something put you on one side of a precipice looking over the chasm at what you truly desire. Action, doing, and working act as a bridge over that chasm and get you to the other side. Action speaks louder than all the words in the English language. American industrialist Andrew Carnegie said, "As I grow older, I pay less attention to what men say. I just watch what they do."

What do your actions say about you?

Talking is Easy, Doing is Hard

Two cars waited, one in front of the other, at a traffic light. The light turned green, but the man in the lead car did not notice it. A woman in the car behind him began pounding on her steering wheel and yelling at the man to move. The man just sat there. The woman was enraged and began ranting and raving at the man, pounding on her steering wheel and dash. The light turned yellow and the car sat. The woman pounded on the car's horn, continually flipping the man her middle finger and hurling four letter words at the man. The driver in the lead car, hearing the commotion, looked up, saw the yellow light and accelerated through the intersection just as the light turned red. The woman was beside herself screaming in frustration. As she is in mid-rant with some colorful four letter word combinations, she heard a tap on her window and looked up into the barrel of a gun held by a very serious looking policeman. The policeman commanded her to shut off her car while keeping both hands in plain sight. She complied, speechless at what was happening. After she shut off the engine, the policeman ordered her to exit her car with her hands up. She got out, was hand-cuffed and hustled into the patrol car. The woman was too bewildered to ask any questions and was driven in silence to the police station where she was fingerprinted, photographed, searched, booked and placed in a cell. After a few hours, a policeman opened the cell door and escorted her to the booking desk where the arresting officer was waiting for her. The policeman looked sheepish and began, "*I am terribly sorry Ma'am for this unfortunate incident.*" The woman placed her hands on her hips in a show of indignation and started to lay into the policeman, but he continued. "You see, Ma'am, I pulled up behind your car and noticed the *Choose God!* license plate holder, the *What Would Jesus Do?* and *Follow Me to Sunday School* bumper stickers and the chrome-plated Christian fish emblem on the trunk, so when I saw someone blaring the horn, cursing a blue streak and flipping that guy off I knew you *must have stolen the car.*"

The woman wanted everyone to think she was one thing, yet her actions told another story.

What story does the way you live tell about you?

Merck Pharmaceuticals is a large international corporation with well-known drugs like Vioxx, Singulair, Zocor, and Propecia. It is a powerful multi-billion dollar corporation which, in its more than three hundred year history, developed a long list of important drugs and established a core set of values. The company's mission statement appears in all internal company documents, is part of the décor of the company's many offices and research facilities, and is learned by each new employee around the world.

Many years ago Merck was faced with a *walk the talk* dilemma. The folks in research and development created a new drug with the ability to end a little known disease called *onchocerciasis*—river blindness. The dilemma occurred when Merck announced to the African countries in which the disease appears a drug was now available to end their people's suffering. The governments from those countries were *under whelmed*. "We are happy you have created this drug," they said, "*but we do not have any money to buy it.*" Merck was deflated by the realization there was no market for their new drug Mectizan; they could make no money from it. Someone, however, pointed to the first of the company's corporate values: *Our business is preserving and improving human life.* So, Merck gave the Mectizan to the African countries free of charge. The African governments replied, "*Great! Thank you, but we do not have doctors to administer the drugs.*"

Merck, again reminded of their company's mission statement, offered to send doctors to Africa without charge to administer the free drug. "*Wonderful,*" said the Africans, "*But we do not have trucks to take the doctors and drugs to the extremely remote areas where river blindness occurs.*" Merck sent the drugs to cure the disease, doctors to administer the drugs, and trucks to carry it all with no thought of profit. They did so because it was part of their core organizational values. Merck put its principles into action and recently administered the 250 millionth free dose of Mectizan in Africa.

Talking is easy, doing is hard. Creating a drug to end someone's suffering is no good unless those suffering have access to the drug. Merck understood this and did the tough and costly things that fulfilled their principles and values. To be a person of good character you must, as Eleanor Roosevelt advised, "Do the things you think you cannot do."

Fred Selfe walked his talk each day. Like Nathan Graybeal's comments about anonymously shoveling snow for the elderly, or his sense of duty in erecting the playground for Nancy Hockett, Fred Selfe had the courage to do the things others only talk about.

Nancy's mother, Belle Hockett, tells this story. "One of the winters when Leo was so sick there was a big snow at Emory. I stepped outside to do something leaving Leo inside by himself when Fred called to check on him. Leo was pretty weak and I guess Fred heard it in his voice. A little while later there came Fred and Becky. He had walked through the snow and she skied to get all the way to our house. Fred moved snow away from the tractor— got the truck free, pulled it up to the front door and made a way for us to get Leo to the hospital. He even drove us there and stayed for hours to take us home again. I guess he could have just called 911 and been done with it, even though they wouldn't have been able to reach us. Instead, he saw what needed to be done and did it."

In the early 1980s offensive lineman Bob Maynard's father passed away and Coach Selfe got the message first. He could have sent someone else to tell Bob, but instead chose to do his duty as a coach and carried it himself. "We were just about ready to leave for Christmas break in December 1982, when I saw something completely out of the ordinary; Coach Selfe and Bruce Hatch coming up the Hillman dorm steps. It was strange to see them because coaches normally never came around the dorms. When Coach Selfe stopped at my door, I had a strange feeling something was just not right. What happened in the next few moments changed my life forever. Coach Selfe put his hand on my shoulder, looked me square in the eye and said, 'I've got some tough news for you, partner.' He then told me my Dad had passed away. He stood there without taking his hand off my shoulder and let me get it all out before telling me about the arrangements for me to get back to Roanoke. As I reflect back almost 22 years later, I realize just how difficult that assignment must have been to carry out. I can only now appreciate what Coach Selfe did on that December evening in 1982. I guess after 18 years of coaching, I can start to appreciate the compassion a coach can have for their players. I know it was not easy for him to stand in that dorm room and tell me of my Dad's death. I have been blessed over the years to coach young people in the sport I love, and his influence on me allowed to me pass on to my players those things he felt were important: integrity, honesty, and intensity."

Maynard teaches and coaches in Big Rapids, Michigan and says he works each day to be more like Fred Selfe. "My respect for Coach Selfe will never waiver because of his example as a man of character. There are certain people who, when you look back on your life, you know they were, and are, a major influence on the path you have taken. Coach Selfe is definitely one of those people."

He did not merely talk about helping others, he did it. I heard many stories like Belle Hockett's about the small things he did for people; students, neighbors, friends and strangers. As Mrs. Hockett declared, "he saw what needed to be done and did it." In a special college *Alumni* magazine article his daughter, Paige Selfe McCauley, says of her father, "He received great pleasure from giving. It didn't matter to whom; he just liked giving to someone. He had great stories of taking underprivileged children to buy shoes, helping a neighbor who was an alcoholic, rescuing a student, or restoring the roof on a home of someone who did not have the funds to do it themselves. He was unbelievably non-judgmental and found good in everyone—no matter how rotten the rest of society viewed them."

His friend and fellow player, Gary Hall relates in the same article, "Fred, without a doubt, was the most remarkable person I have ever known. He was always quiet and reserved, consistent in his character, respectful to all he came into contact with. He was the epitome of all things good in mankind—honest, humble, intelligent, tireless, and loyal. He was an exemplary leader in all that he did, and as Doug Reavis said at the memorial service, 'Coach Selfe taught me so much and he did it by example, without ever saying a word.' I can honestly say I have never known any human being I respected more."

Mike Griffith calls him a "man's man" who "did not lead by talk, he lead by example—a person of deep character. One who would have made a great head coach, at any level, but he was not a political man." He was devoted to helping others and a super mentor to those young men who played for him."

Bruce Hatch agrees, "He led by example while demonstrating pride, devotion, and excellence. In short, he represented everything that Emory and Henry wants to say about itself and wants for its students."

In fact, the theme of Fred Selfe exemplifying the themes the college considers its values as an institution of higher learning is a common one. The Rev. David St. Clair, Emory and Henry Class of 1973, referred to this theme at the memorial service, saying Fred Selfe embodied the college's Latin motto, *Macte Virtute—Increase in Excellence*.

Emory and Henry College has veered little from its founding values—the values of the "wild border democracy" it serves. Professor George J. Stevenson reports in his book *Increase in Excellence, a History of Emory and Henry College*, an 1839 visitor to the college, James Silk Buckingham described the school as a manual labor institute designed after Emmanuel von Fellenberg's school at Hoffwyl, Switzerland. Stevenson claims the founders believed the school "located in a prosperous, developing region might contribute to the further economic and social development of the region. It would be a cultural asset for an area not otherwise endowed with such benefits." In the preface of the book Stevenson defines the college's original and lasting values as these: "*Emory and Henry College is a product of the contrapuntal themes of denominationalism and democracy characteristic of the 1830s. Its purpose was to further the premise that theology is the foundation of knowledge. Without apology it has maintained that position for 125 years, surviving the vicissitudes that caused many of its contemporaries to founder, maintaining it place is higher education in the face of increasing competition from secular institutions, and exemplifying the continuing tradition of the small liberal arts college.*"

Methodism is widely regarded as a *mission-based* sect of the Protestant faith with a long history of lay preachers and circuit riders going out into the countryside to extol the virtues of Wesleyan theology. In fact, one of Emory and Henry's most famous students, future Confederate cavalry commander J.E.B. Stuart was swept up in one of the traveling Methodist tent revivals while in attendance at the college. According to H.B McClellan's *Life and Campaigns of Major-General J.E.B. Stuart*, "At the age of 14 years James Stuart was placed at school in Wytheville; and in August, 1848, he entered Emory and Henry College. During a revival of religion among the students he professed conversion, and joined the Methodist Church."

Hard work, religious conviction, civic virtue, superior teaching and learning, contributing to cultural value, and service to others are summed up by the motto *Increase in Excellence* and most surely personified by Fred Dean Selfe. He, as the Rev. St. Clair, Bruce Hatch, Bob Johnson and I believe, *is* Emory and Henry College. As Carter Moore writes in the college's online news website *EHC Wired*, "The character of the college is measured by the character of its students, faculty and staff." Those of us proud of our alma mater and true believers in those shared values wait to see how the college chooses to honor Fred Selfe: re-naming a major building or the football field, erecting a large statue, establishing a center for civic leadership—the college certainly has a wonderful opportunity to show the world *who* Emory and Henry is by honoring Fred Selfe in a lasting and tangible way.

Dave Thomas, Assistant Coach in Charge of Equipment and Facilities, died shortly after Fred Selfe from cancer. For many years, Dave cared for the King Athletic Center and kept the equipment clean and safe for the college's sports teams. He and Coach Selfe worked closely together and forged a solid friendship. "Coach Selfe was truly an angel among us," Thomas said. "He touched the lives of those who loved him so many ways and we were blessed to have him as a friend for so many years. When I found out I had leukemia, he was one of the first people to find out. From that point on, he stood behind me through the sickness and through the treatments. I have never met someone who was so unselfish, so willing to help anyone in need, and always ready to offer his love and support. The world has lost a noble saint."

In 2001 a young player was badly injured in an inter-squad scrimmage. Danny Carter, a defensive back from Blountville, Tennessee displaced a vertebra leaving him paralyzed. It hit Fred Selfe hard too. He camped out at the hospital with the family, constantly called to check on Danny's condition and, according to Becky Selfe, lost night after night of sleep worrying and grieving about Danny. He wrote in a letter to Jim Ballard, who was on the first team Fred Selfe coached in 1973, that the terrible injury was something no one could have foreseen, yet he seemed haunted by it. "Never in my wildest fears did I anticipate the actuality of the neck injury to Danny. I sincerely pray for his full recovery." He drove an hour each day to pick up Danny and bring him to the college to be among other students so he would not be isolated and might regain some degree of normalcy. He willed Danny to keep up his strength and his optimism. Becky Selfe says he felt a deep sense of duty to keep Danny from losing hope. In fact, his dying wish was for those who would memorialize him through flowers or other material things instead send contributions to the Danny Carter Medical Benefit Fund. "That's just like Fred," ODAC commissioner Brad Bankston says, "Even at the end he wanted to do something for someone else."

Danny Carter is cautiously improving. He spent months in the Spinal Cord Restorative Treatment and Research Program at the Washington University School of Medicine and recently moved with his family to California to join an experimental program that focuses on strength training and diet. He has realized some movement returning to his upper body and arms and doctors are optimistic about his continued improvement. Danny writes about his admiration for Coach Selfe and his powerful influence in a letter to Becky Selfe: "Some people become friends and sometimes they become great friends. Coach was a great friend. He left his footprint on my heart forever. I often ask myself 'What would Coach do?' when times are tough. I know he would always have the right answer. From the moment I stepped foot on Emory's campus, Coach Selfe was there to guide me. Whether it was trying to find the cafeteria or my football locker, he was there. After I got hurt he was still there. Mom and Dad call him an angel. I call him my dearest friend. Coach, I'm going to walk for you *Dagnabbit!*"

Coach Selfe never stopped believing he would.

FIVE GREAT BIG SMALL THINGS

1) *As Iron Sharpens Iron*, Your Life Can Sharpen So Many Others
2) Beat Your Wings
3) Be Courageous and Contagious
4) Build a Strong House
5) Put Your Principles Into Action

Act now. Stop thinking about and talking about being a better person and get to it. Take Mahatma Gandhi's advice, "Be the change you want to see in the world." Use the lessons of Fred Selfe for getting things done and doing for others to bridge the gap between wanting and being.

Stop making plans and make tracks. Walk your talk. Once you do, you will wake up each morning and greet the person you wish to see in the mirror.

Put your principles into action.

SIXTH
GREAT BIG
SMALL THING

15-and-3 Leadership

Leadership must be based on goodwill. Goodwill does not mean posturing and, least of all, pandering to the mob. It means obvious and wholehearted commitment to helping followers. We are tired of leaders we fear, tired of leaders we love, and of tired of leaders who let us take liberties with them. What we need for leaders are men of the heart who are so helpful that they, in effect, do away with the need of their jobs. But leaders like that are never out of a job, never out of followers. Strange as it sounds, great leaders gain authority by giving it away.

Admiral James B. Stockdale

Control is not leadership; management is not leadership; Leadership is leadership. If you seek to lead, invest at least 50 percent of your time in leading yourself—your own purpose, ethics, principles, motivation, conduct. Invest at least 20 percent leading those with authority over you and 15 percent leading your peers.

Dee Hock, Founder of Visa

Our culture suffers from a scarcity of leadership. Not a lack of people in positions of power—power attracts people like moths to the flame—rather we are running a deficit of *good people* at the heads of our flocks. Simply put, many people in leadership positions today lack the traits of quality leaders. These organizations, and those whom they serve, suffer dearly for it.

Our confidence in the traditional foundations of our culture has eroded to the point where we have no faith in each other or even ourselves. And who can blame us? Let me give you some credible statistics to prove this point and a larger one: A recent *USA Today* survey found 82 percent of corporate CEOs admitted to cheating at golf. Most people may not recognize the significance of something as small as fudging a missed putt here and there, but consider for a moment what occurred recently with Enron, WorldCom, Tyco, HealthSouth, and Martha Stewart. Remember my client who thought she was organized in her *business life* even if she was disorganized in her *private life*? You cannot compartmentalize your life. The way you are is the way you are. Those CEOs—the men and women who carry the titles—were simply not worthy of our trust. If they cheat at golf, odds are, they cheat in business.

The 2003 Harris Interactive Confidence Index, a national survey based on confidence in the leaders of major cultural institutions, shows a slightly above-average 57 percent confidence in the strength of the pillars of our culture: The U.S. military, White House, Supreme Court, and major educational institutions. Our confidence and trust in these societal bodies is lost because we have been constantly disappointed by the leaders of these organizations. Take a look at the very bottom of the list. Those in whom we have the least confidence are the leaders of major companies (13 percent), Wall Street (12 percent), law firms (12 percent), and organized labor (14 percent).

Richard Yukubousky, Executive Director of the Municipal Research and Services Center, a non-profit organization offering research and information on all aspects of civic and community life for the cities and towns of Washington State, says his organization finds, "Lower rates of civic participation have also reduced the pool of people who learn how to run meetings, speak in public, organize projects, and debate public projects with civility. And this is the same pool of citizens from which we have traditionally drawn most of our civic leaders. The result has been fewer citizens who are willing or able to participate in their communities' civic affairs."

The human deficit Yukubousky uncovered is not unique to Washington State but endemic to our entire country. The larger point I mentioned is *good leaders are rare as a white buffalo*. The lack of good leadership—or the replacement of it by bad leadership—saps our confidence in our institutions which, in turn, decreases our participation in them. Americans would rather cocoon in their homes than join a social or service organization led by people they cannot trust. A recent article in

Rotarian magazine, the Rotary Club's publication, reports its own membership down considerably, Lions Club membership down by 12 percent since 1983, Shriners by 32 percent, and Jaycees by 44 percent.

Separately, we note a major decline in membership in social and civic organizations, an abysmal confidence level in societal institutions, and, as a Gallup Poll reports, "Seven in 10 people claim religious membership, yet in the past 30 years, the number of Americans who attend weekly services has generally hovered at only 40 percent of Americans." What does it all mean when we see it together?

These elements are called our *social capital.* According to the World Bank, "Social capital refers to the institutions, relationships, and norms that shape the quality and quantity of a society's social interactions. Social capital is not just the sum of the institutions which underpin a society–it is the glue that holds them together." So then, if our culture is coming undone, does that not mean the glue is failing, and if the glue is not working can it not be theorized it is because we lack the chemical bonds that give the glue strength? Good leaders are the bonds that hold our social institutions together and help them expand and work to complete their missions. Without those bonds, or worse when the bonds are *bad*, we come apart at the seams. Good leadership is essential to keeping our culture together.

Some claim the attributes of leadership are subjective—up to anyone's interpretation. I am a contrarian to that view. I argue there are *15 tried and true characteristics* that, by consensus, make for good leaders and conversely explain their scarcity:

15 TRIED AND TRUE CHARACTERISTICS OF GOOD LEADERS

1.   Courageous

Good leaders are willing to stand alone and risk failure. The challenges they take on, thinking them the right thing to do, may turn away the faint of heart—no matter—they make the stand. Like Mike Griffith's story of being dragged by Fred Selfe to the college president's office to make a pitch for higher pay for the football coaches; it was not the easy thing to do, but it was the *right* thing. He rarely saw a situation and thought it impossible. Fred Selfe lived each day with the courage to stand alone—without care for what others thought. He did the right things each and every day out of habit.

2.   Live with integrity

Good leaders are ethical. They have firm, fixed beliefs and do not wander from them. Good leaders are the people to whom we turn in times of trouble and upheaval. Fred

Selfe was a rock of integrity. Every single person I interviewed, or who contributed to this book, says he was a man of great character. Most people, like Gary Hall, say they have not known anyone they respect more. His integrity was so impressive it was studied, learned and imitated by legions of men and women. An Emory and Henry student who did not play sports says Fred Selfe was the most impressive thing he encountered on the campus. "He was the greatest man I've ever met face to face. I always knew I could look to him to know what to do and how to do it." Danny Carter says Fred Selfe helped him understand the very ideal of character: "Sometimes people come into your life and you know right away they were meant to be there; to serve some sort of purpose. Teach you a lesson or help figure out who you are or want to become. You never know who these people may be, but when you lock eyes with them you know that very moment they will affect your life in some profound way. Sometimes things happen to you at a time that may seem horrible, painful and unfair, but in reflection you realize that without overcoming these obstacles you would have never realized your potential, strength, or will power. Everything happens for a reason. Nothing happens by chance or by means of good luck, illness or injury. All occur to test the limits of your soul."

3.   Accountable

Good leaders take responsibility for their decisions and actions—both good and bad. They recognize their duty as a leader and hold themselves accountable for the success or failure of the group they lead. Fred Selfe shouldered the blame for every loss his team encountered over the 29 years he coached. He made tough choices and boldly stood behind each one. Good leaders also give the credit to others. Dr. Thomas Morris, Emory and Henry's current president says, "He would not take credit for his accomplishments, but he would always give credit for their accomplishments. In that way he made himself a unique person for this day and age where others clamor to get credit for what they do." Coach Bob Johnson says Selfe was an ideal leader: "He wasn't particularly concerned with covering his back. He didn't deflect responsibility. If a kid missed a block, dropped a pass, fumbled or showed up to a practice late, Fred took the blame. When a kid succeeded in some way because of his tutelage, Fred would congratulate the student and then disappear before taking any of the credit. He led from the front and after the completion of the job he stood in the rear and let others take the credit."

4.   Sacrifice personal interests

Good leaders take care of the group's needs first and themselves second. One student wrote to Coach Self during his illness: "It is so inappropriate your name is Selfe—because you are the most *self-less* person I've ever known." Almost every evening around 10:00pm Fred and Becky Selfe jumped into the car, drove to campus and checked all the doors at the King Athletic Center to make sure they were secure. He felt it his responsibility—even though campus security was in charge of locking the doors to all campus buildings—and it came before his own comfort, he felt it his duty. He mowed, sowed, limed and led the crews that did all the work on getting the practice and game fields ready for his teams. He was the first to the hospital when a player was rushed there for an injury, usually driving the player home and lending words of encouragement. Phillip Henley says he awoke from emergency knee surgery following an accident in a baseball game to find Coach Selfe "starring down at me in the recovery room." Henley continues, "During the eight days I was in the hospital, Coach Selfe took time away from his teaching, coaching and family to visit each day." He did these things without concern for his own comfort and interests. Coach Steve Allen says, "There are times when I'm standing around the athletic department washing machine washing some kid's clothes at 11:30 at night and I think of Coach Selfe. He did that kind of selfless work—laundry, building things, cleaning, mowing—year round for 26 years . . . he gave and gave and gave. Most people don't know how much he gave because he never once asked for thanks or made himself more important than the job."

5.   Optimists

They see the good in every situation and help others see it too. They are like the second person in the story from the book *The Art of Possibility*:

> A shoe factory executive sends two marketing scouts to a remote region of Africa to study the prospects for expanding business.
>
> One sends back a message saying, *"Situation hopeless. No one wears shoes."*
>
> The other writes back triumphantly, ***"Glorious business opportunity. They have no shoes."***

Fred Selfe saw the good in all people and situations. His daughter Paige says he found the good in everyone "no matter how rotten the rest of society viewed them." Bronwyn Reynolds tells of his unwavering belief she could play basketball for Emory and Henry when other colleges and people turned her away because of her diminished height. "Being a 'munchkin' (a nickname given her by Coach Selfe) only five-feet-tall no one ever believed I would play college basketball anywhere," she says. "E&H believed in me when no one else did, and so did Coach Selfe. He didn't believe in the things you couldn't do. He believed in making the best of what you could do and enhancing the positive qualities that you possess, making goals and playing your hardest to achieve those goals." It takes courage to know you are right and act on those beliefs.

Bob Johnson tells a story to illustrate Coach Selfe's physical strength, but it says something about how he viewed the world: "I say 'Freddy, you need to help me to get this piano from so-and-so's house to my house.' I said, 'what do you need?' He said, 'why don't you bring four or five guys over.' Okay, I get four or five guys and we go get the piano. I say, 'Hey Freddy, where do you want us?' He says, you guys get on that end and I'll get this end.' True story—he lifts half the piano by himself." The newly-purchased piano Bob Johnson needed to move was a challenge, but like Archimedes, all Fred Selfe needed was a place to stand and he could move the world.

6.   Coup d'oeil

Good leaders have a talent known as *coup d'oeil* (koo dwee); the ability to glance at a situation and see it in its entirety. Hannibal used it at the battle of Cannae, Naploeon at Toulon, Robert E. Lee at Chancellorsville. It is a kind of clear vision unclouded by doubt or reservation. It is one of the attributes that made Fred Selfe a successful offensive coordinator. He could size up a defense and find their weaknesses at a glance. He could do the same with situations and people; perhaps because he had so much faith in his own judgment.

Dr. Paul Blaney, Dean of Faculty at Emory and Henry, says about Fred Selfe, "What struck me most was his apparent ability to figure out what to do and then do it on the spot. His lightening speed arose from his unusual clarity about right and wrong . . . ."

You have coup d'oeil, you may just call it your *intuition*. When you see a situation, perhaps not as large as Napoleon faced at Toulon, you have an intuitive sense of what it means and what could happen. That is a weak form of coup d'oeil. Learn to trust it and strengthen it. Learn to use it.

7.   Strive for excellence not perfection

Good leaders know perfection is like a vacuum in science or full employment in economics—it simply does not exist in the natural world. Instead of pushing people toward this unreachable goal they help them strive for excellence in their actions. As Temple Musser points out, Fred Selfe could take good players and turn them into great players. He did not expect them to be perfect lineman, just excellent linemen. Those linemen worked harder not to disappoint their "Daddy". The Old Dominion Athletic Conference is a group of small colleges with young athletes playing sports for the love of the game: Washington and Lee, Catholic, Randolph-Macon, Hampden-Sydney, Bridgewater, Roanoke, Guilford, Lynchburg, Hollins, Sweet Briar, Eastern Mennonite, and Virginia Wesleyan. There are no scholarships, just hard work and hard play. Coach Selfe knew the majority of the young student-athletes will never go on to the professional level—they are getting degrees to go out into the world to teach, treat patients, do research, report news, and earn advanced degrees. They give their time and effort for the glory of the college and a chance to bring pride to the blue and gold uniform. He coached and taught with respect for that loyalty. He pushed players to learn the best practices and do them time and again—to get better each time out until they played with excellence. That type of coaching helped create 37 All-American football players in the last 20 years.

8.   Stay *on mission*

Good leaders know the goal. They accept and *own* it. It becomes the single thing on which they focus. You will understand this if you ever encountered Fred Selfe on a game week. It was all about *that* game. Not the season in general, but whichever team we were playing the coming Saturday. He kept us focused and ready to play the team that week. College is a place of constant distractions— classes, clubs, fraternities and sororities—it is a non-stop, chaotic world. Throw in a sport and time becomes a rare commodity. Coach Selfe kept us focused on the task at hand. He started immediately following the most recent game. On any given Sunday we would gather in the King Center to watch the film of yesterday's game and Coach Selfe would shift the focus from the performance we were there to see to the next team's defense and how we might defeat it. When mistakes were made he pushed us past them and got our minds refocused on the bigger goal.

9.　Serve

Good leaders are what Robert K. Greenleaf, former Director of Management and Research for AT&T, calls *servant-leaders*. He coined the phrase to describe those people who choose to serve first then lead as a way of expanding service to individuals and institutions. It is a hallmark of good leaders to recognize they lead not for themselves, but for those who follow them. The entire next section of this book is about servant leadership and how Fred Selfe served the world. Josh Wellenhoffer, a former *Wasp* lineman, says, "My parents are divorced— my dad lives in Utah and my mom in South Carolina. I did have a dad near me and his name was Fred Selfe. He took me under his wing and watched out for me. When he passed away I lost a loved one. As I grow older I want to change and when I change I want to change into Coach Selfe and care for everyone."

10.　Empower others:
　　Trust your teammates. Trust yourself

Good leaders teach others to teach. They give their followers a clear and concise vision of the mission—the *whys* and *hows*—AND the power to get it done. Good leaders "put power into" the hands of each person working for the goal. Fred Selfe turned good players into great players by empowering them to play their positions and play as a team.

Chris Musser, a former *Wasp* football and baseball player, tells a story of coming back to the college as an assistant baseball coach in 1990: "I was pulling my hair out on the bench after one game. Coach Selfe came and sat down next to me and said only this, 'You can't catch it for them or throw it for them or hit it for them. *Prepare them as well as you can and let them play.*' Then he patted me on the knee and got up and walked to the gym. That is something I have never forgotten, and, for me anyway, it kind of keeps things in perspective."

Empowering others means giving them the tools, training, respect, guidance, and care they need to succeed. It is also about clearly defining the goals and the parameters they have in which to operate. Empowerment is about approaching every situation as a partnership—a team effort. My senior year we got new uniforms. My first three years we wore old, worn out pants and jerseys. Dave Thomas had bleached the old, white game pants so much they were stiff and scratchy. They were so stiff, I once had our two best defensive linemen, Rob McMillan and J.D. Washington, hold my pair and I climbed up on a bench to lower myself into them. These two big buys held the pants as I wriggled, pushed and shoved myself down into the legs. Just as I had them almost completely on they ripped apart and fell to shreds.

We came in from practice one Thursday to find the brand-spanking new uniforms hanging in our lockers. Bright yellow pants and blue jerseys hung there like ornaments on a Christmas tree. There was silence in a locker room where 100 young men usually talked and laughed so loudly you could barely hear the person next to you. Coach Selfe came around taking them out of the lockers and making sure they fit each player. He was beaming with pride. We were mesmerized by the new uniforms, and I think he was more proud than any of us. He was not going to wear one of the uniforms, but his boys were and that made him so happy he could barely contain himself. I also remember him pointing out that each pair of pants had a private label sewn inside with the name of the Los Angeles Ram on them. These pants were supposed to be headed for an NFL star, but somehow made it into our lockers. He and Coach Wacker (and some hard working local alums) gave us new tools to play better football. Coach Selfe was as excited as I have ever seen him because he knew how excited we would be and how that would positively affect our performance It did—we were ODAC champs, played in the NCAA Division III playoffs and ended the season with a record of ten wins and only two losses.

Rodney Beville, an exceptional, fast and clever running back shares this story about the trust Fred Selfe had in his players: "In baseball, we mostly played doubleheaders. One day we were playing Eastern Mennonite and before the game I was talking to one of their players. This player knew we had a good football team and said he was thinking about transferring so he could play for us. I mentioned the football team had a high standard to live up to. It just so happened this guy pitched the first game of the doubleheader. He was very animated on the mound—cursing, throwing things around and mouthing to other player—not good baseball etiquette. We won the game, but his antics did not sit well with me. At the end of the second game, I told my teammates—some of them football players too—to get behind me in the line as we shook hands with the other team. When I got to the pitcher, I shook his hand and asked, "Are you still planning to transfer here to play football?" He said, 'Yes.' I told him 'Don't! We don't need *a___holes* like you on our team.' I kept shaking hands and looked back to see a pushing and shoving match had broken out. The next day at our team meeting before practice Coach Selfe said, 'I don't know *what* was said yesterday or *who* said it'— silence hung in the air—'but I agree . . . .' Coach Selfe never said anything directly to me about that incident, but what he showed me was that Emory is a family . . . that we will take care of that family, and we will do what is right for that family. By not reprimanding me, he showed faith and trust that I would do what was best for the family we call Emory and Henry."

11. Have deep concern for others and treat them with respect and dignity

Good leaders are caring people. They have a deep and real concern for others. They have a clear understanding that their team—family, group, school, organization, company, neighborhood, church, or synagogue—is made up of individuals and the well-being of each individual affects the team's overall performance. Good leaders genuinely care about the people who follow them. Another well known trait is how Fred Selfe addressed people either by their jersey number or Mister or Missus. "All rigthty, Mr. Dean, get out there and find that linebacker." "Hello Miss Williams." "You're NOT actually considering this are you, Miss Hockett?" It was an impressive thing for a coach to address me "Mr. McGlothlin" as a freshman. It left an indelible mark on me by making me feel respected. I found I acted in kind.

Joe Cundiff, a former Graham High School (Bluefield, Virginia) standout and E&H quarterback in the late 1980s, and I coached a little league football team one season in Johnson City, Tennessee. It was a real challenge to work with the nine, ten, and 11-year-old kids from one of the poorest neighborhoods of the city, but we decided to do it like Coach Selfe. We changed everything. We treated them with respect, called them Mister and their last names, taught them to teach each other the plays in our limited playbook, and we blocked off the two hour practice to one hour of football and one hour tutoring them with their homework. We came onto the field and warmed up with no fanfare, in fact we did not say a word. Plus, in true Coach Selfe style, we allowed no "hotdogging" or "grandstanding" of any kind. It was all about working as a team and doing your job.

In the YMCA league, one coach is in the huddle to put the kids in their positions and tell them where to go one each play—basically placing the kids where they need be and telling them each play what to do. Joe worked with the offense to the point where he was calling in the plays from the sidelines with hand signals amazing the referees and other coaches. Our little team, the Raiders—a team that had been last in the league the previous year and abandoned by its coach just two weeks before the season began—played in the finals and lost the championship game by a single touchdown.

Fred Selfe respected everyone. It was the kind of general respect for humankind found in Doug Reavis' story about the dirty, disheveled man he saw wandering around campus he thought might be a vagrant, or even worse, dangerous. Coach Selfe went right up to him, put his hand on the man's shoulder and said, "Hello Mr. So-and-So! "How are things going? Still holding up? You got enough wood? Do you need me to get you some more?" Pat Walker says in an article in the *Bristol Herald-Courier* newspaper, "I grew up without a father and Coach Selfe filled that role better than anyone ever did. I was 18 when I first met him. From day one he treated me with respect. He has always made it clear he cared about me as a person, not just a football player. That fact alone sets him apart from the rest of the world."

12.   Listen

There is a Turkish proverb, "If speaking is silver, then listening is gold." Good leaders know how much that *gold* is truly worth.

In 1995 I was CEO of a book publishing company and we were considering publishing a work by a writer in Scottsdale, Arizona based on her self-improvement teachings. The subject held some interest, so I decided to take one of her weekend workshops called *The Listening Course* to judge the potential of marketing the book. On the first day of the course we got into groups of five people and were tasked to tell the group about the worst experience of our lives. Sounds pretty simple, but the following caveats were added: First, we had five minutes to tell the story. If we finished before the five minutes were up we had to sit in silence. Second, the listeners could not speak, nod their heads or in any way interrupt the speaker. We had to sit very still and pay close attention to the person telling the story. I, and my fellow team members, learned some very important things from that exercise: Five minutes is an eternity. The first woman told her story in two minutes and without much detail or emotion, so we were forced to sit in uncomfortable silence for what seemed forever waiting for the next three minutes to tick away. The next person got deeper into the story and gave us more feelings and details. This guy got very close to the five minute mark, but still we had to sit through a minute of silence. I told my story and the five minutes went by fast. The thing I noticed—I felt most—for maybe the first time in a long while, was what it was like to be heard. I knew, absolutely knew, those four people were hearing what I was saying. They were focused on me—not thinking about what they would say next. They were hearing everything I was saying and that confidence led me to tell more and more of the complete story without realizing it. I was still telling the story when my five minutes were up. Being heard is a very powerful thing.

I heard this interesting story a few years ago from a best-selling author. A young man working on his PhD. in sociology gets on a one-and-a-half-hour airplane flight and engages the person sitting next to him in conversation for the entire flight. One of his rules is to tell as little about himself as he can get away with. Once the plane lands a team stops and interviews the other passenger about the man. His research showed two amazing things: the passenger thought the man the most interesting person they'd met, AND they knew nothing about him—not his name, profession, age, home—nothing. Because the man let them talk about *themselves*, HE was the most interesting man they had ever met.

Fred Selfe listened. He was an active listener, asking questions and drilling down into comments to get more information. He heard what you said and captured it. It was about you because he made it about you. His use of the formal address *Mister* or *Missus* and his active listening made me feel he respected and cared for my concerns. In turn, I respected him more and worked harder to please him. When I would see him, whether it was the next football season or ten football seasons, he knew my name, my jersey number, and asked about my job and my parents. As Bruce Hatch remarked, it was important to him for his players to do well.

13.   Reward great performers

Good leaders make sure they reward great performers. Top, or peak performance, is the goal of preparing to play a sport. Anyone can put out mediocre play; it is the comfort zone and path of least resistance I mentioned earlier. Getting out of that zone and outperforming what you think are the limits of your abilities is the difference in a good player and a great player. Coach Selfe built great players. His rewards, or motivation, were both extrinsic and intrinsic. Extrinsically he patted you on the back, called out your name with an energetic *Gosh Dandy* thrown in somewhere, shook your hand or, as he did me, took you by the shoulder pads and shook you like a pork chop in bag of *Shake'n Bake*. He gave you all the credit for what you did right and he did it in front of your teammates. Once a young player experienced that sort of motivation it became an intrinsic one—something we did just for the good feeling we got from it. Pride is an intrinsic reward and Coach Selfe helped his players find that kind of pride in achieving excellence.

14.   Challenge themselves and others

If we lived in a static world, one that never changed, the *status quo* would be good enough. Good leaders know, however, that we live in a chaotic, ever-changing world—a universe in flux. The only constant is change. In our world, as Ronald Reagan put it, "*Status quo . . .* is Latin for *the mess we're in.*" There is always a better way of doing something. As humans we easily become content with comfort and move toward the path of least resistance. There is no guarantee that path leads in the right direction. Good leaders expose this. They push us to get off that path and find a better, straighter one. Oft time the good path is steeper and more arduous, but good leaders make sure it is the right one to be trekking and help us stay on it.

Pat Walker tells this story of how Coach Selfe cared for him, nurtured him and challenged him by "putting me *in position to have a positive outcome.*" Pat says, "I went to Emory for five years and two summer schools . . . changed majors three times. During my third year I went to my advisor and told him I wanted to teach economics in high school. This was a big step for me because I had no confidence in myself except on the football field. Well, the advisor laughed at me. I got up and ran from his office— absolutely crushed. I went back to my dorm room and cried. I called coach Selfe, still crying. He told me to come on down to the King Center. We went for a ride in his little pickup and he bought me a hotdog from a little place in Glade Springs. We just rode around . . . most of all he listened to me. He was there for me . . . he cared about me. After I calmed down we went to his office and he asked, 'What is it you want to do more than anything else?' I told him I always wanted to teach P.E. and coach football, but I didn't pursue it because I was not encouraged by my family. He sent me back to my room and told me to come back at a certain time the next day assuring me things would work out. When I came back the next day, Coach Selfe had planned my next two years (and another summer school) AND become my advisor. He was going to help me become the P.E. teacher I wanted to be. I was mostly an underachieving student up to that point, but after I made the dean's list every semester. I finished as the top senior in the P.E. department my last year . . . got an award and everything. Now, here's the thing: I wanted to please him so badly he got me to work at my *maximum ability*, and that led to whatever success I have. What I didn't realize at the time was 'he was just putting me in position to have a positive outcome' as he liked to say. I looked at it as 'I'm pleasing Coach.' He looked at it as, *'look at what that boy can do when someone believes in him.'* Along the way, I began to believe in myself as much as he believed in me."

People did more for Coach Selfe because he asked them or expected it. He pushed himself and he pushed us. Like French painter Guillaume Apollinare's quote, "he coaxed us toward the edge then pushed us off—*and we flew.*"

Fred Selfe was a natural leader. He rarely asked others to follow, but instead he did what he thought right and attracted followers because he deserved to be followed. As I recounted in preceding chapters, he was a strongly principled man who acted on those principles each day. People followed him because they trusted him—they trusted him because he led by example—and his example was that of a good man.

15.   Keep it simple

Good leaders take complex ideas or challenges and find a way to get to the root of it. They see, define, and act with bold strokes. As Joseph L. Badarracco Jr. writes about leaders, "[They] are usually unencumbered by the technical complexities that permeate so much of life and work today. The Alamo was defended by a handful of men using simple weapons; President Lincoln didn't have an army of lawyers vet the Emancipation Proclamation; and Ann Sullivan didn't have to seek third-party reimbursement before working with Helen Keller."

Fred Selfe was a simple man. He turned seemingly complex situation into simple decisions and simple actions. His powerful offense was broken down into *if this happens do this . . . if not do this scenarios.* On the play *31 Speed* if the corner comes up take him—if not—keep on trucking and block the first man to show up outside the end. It is 15 years since I ran that play but I remember how to run it because of its simple mechanics.

Belle Hockett says once, when her husband Leo was sick and weak, he got up on their house to re-shingle the roof. "Fred Selfe came by, saw Leo up there and walked over to him. He did not try any long, drawn-out arguments, he just asked a simple question, 'You coming down, or am I coming up to get you?" Leo came right down." It cannot be simpler than the speech about responsibility he gave to Joe-Joe Collins, "Make it right!"

THREE *GREAT BIG* LEADERSHIP STYLES

Quiet Leadership

In his book *Leading Quietly*, Badaracco speculates the most effective leaders are not the glamorous, high-status individuals splashed across the headlines, but people who deflect attention and measure their accomplishments through the results of their actions.

Badarracco's book is the result of a four year study conducted of leadership and leaders. In it he writes, "Over the course of a career studying management and leadership, I have observed the most effective leaders are rarely high-profile champions of causes, and don't want to be. They move patiently, carefully, and incrementally. They do what is right—for their organization, for the people around them, and for themselves— inconspicuously and without casualties. I have come to call these people *quiet leaders* because their modesty and restraint are in large measure responsible for their impressive achievements."

Our challenge as a society that, too often, values flash over substance is to recognize those quiet leaders and find ways to support them. I fiercely disagree with English philosopher, Thomas Carlyle, and his theory of the "great man" "sent into the world" as the prime movers of history and change. Carlyle saw leaders as *special people*. People are good leaders not because they are *special*, but are *special* because they are *good leaders*. Each of us is a great man—or woman. We are born with greatness within. All we need do it bring it out.

Our history is moved and shaped by small things—the butterfly's wings of Chaos Theory fame, incrementally, each day doing something good and right. Those wings are so small they are rarely heard by those nearest, but eventually becomes a whirling storm deafening us all with force.

Col. James Moschgat told the U.S. Air Force Academy's graduating class of 1977 a story about his days at the Academy and his squadron's janitor, Bill Crawford. The janitor was a quiet, unassuming man who did his job so well no one noticed him.

"Bill didn't move very quickly and, in fact, you could say he even shuffled a bit, as if he suffered from some sort of injury. His gray hair and wrinkled face made him appear ancient to a group of young cadets. And his crooked smile, well, it looked a little funny. Bill was an old man working in a young person's world."

The 100 or so boys moving at light speed in the dormitory rarely said anything to Bill as he shuffled along cleaning her and there. He was invisible to them. Moschgat remembers that all changed one fateful day in

1976: "I was reading a book about World War II and the tough Allied ground campaign in Italy, when I stumbled across an incredible story. On Sept. 13, 1943, a Private William Crawford from Colorado, assigned to the 36th Infantry Division, had been involved in some bloody fighting on Hill 424 near Altavilla, Italy. The words on the page leapt out at me: '*in the face of intense and overwhelming hostile fire . . . with no regard for personal safety and on his own initiative, Private Crawford single-handedly attacked fortified enemy positions.*" It continued, '*For conspicuous gallantry and intrepidity at risk of life above and beyond the call of duty, the President of the United States . . .* '

'Holy cow,' I said to my roommate, 'you're not going to believe this, but I think our janitor is a Medal of Honor winner.'

The cadets rushed to find Bill and show him the book. "We met Mr. Crawford bright and early Monday and showed him the page in question from the book, anticipation and doubt on our faces. He starred at it for a few silent moments and then quietly uttered something like, 'Yep, that's me.' Mouths agape, my roommate and I looked at one another, then at the book, and quickly back at our janitor. Almost at once we both stuttered, 'Why didn't you ever tell us about it?' He slowly replied after some thought, 'That was one day in my life and it happened a long time ago.' I guess we were all at a loss for words after that." The squadron janitor was a military hero. William "Bill" Crawford was a Medal of Honor recipient.

How many young men noticed Bill before Moschgat discovered the mention of his heroics and valor? None. Mr. Crawford quietly went about living his life and doing his job. As he saw it, his heroism—worthy of our country's highest honor and written into history books—"was one day in my life and it happened a long time ago."

Albert Schweitzer was a quiet servant leader. This famous physician walked away from a promising career in either music or theology each of which would surely have lead to a secure and comfortable life of celebrity. Schweitzer chose instead to serve others through medicine in Africa where it was dangerous and unpleasant. He won the Nobel Prize in 1952 for his long years of humanitarian work with the poor and used the prize money to expand his hospital to treat lepers. Schweitzer wrote in his autobiography, *Out of My Life and Thought*, about the role of simple heroes in our world: "Of all the will toward the ideal in mankind only a small part can manifest itself in public action. All the rest of this force must be content with small and obscure deeds. The sum of these, however, is a thousand times stronger than the acts of those who receive wide public recognition. The latter, compared to the former, are like the foam on the waves of a deep ocean." Schweitzer, an internationally acclaimed physician and Nobel Prize winner, said the small things, "small and obscure deeds," of everyday life are "a thousand times stronger" than those of Carlyle's "*great men*." He calls those high-profile people mere "foam on the waves," the visible part of a deeper, unseen ocean.

Our culture rarely credits people like Bill Crawford and Fred Selfe; men and women who go quietly about their lives leading others to greatness without seeking fame or fortune for themselves. As we swim in the vast ocean, we are touched by the everyday, simple role models of these people who selflessly lift and carry us. We are touched by their acts of kindness, teaching and love.

Quiet leaders are all around us—the undercurrent flowing through our lives. I recently watched documentary after documentary recently as the world celebrated the 60th anniversary of the allied invasion of Europe. The single thread running through the interviews with the men who took part in the invasion was their humility. They are living heroes. They changed the world on June 6, 1944 and the long days that followed. These farm boys, car mechanics, teachers and recent high school graduates beat back the armies of fascism and liberated the peoples of two continents. Everyone living on this earth owes them a debt of gratitude we can never repay. Yet, when they are interviewed about their part in D-Day these men are humble. They shun the spotlight. They say they "were just doing their job." Historian and author Stephen Ambrose, in his book *Citizen Soldiers*, tells how these "sons of democracy" returned from the greatest war in history to marry their sweethearts, build our national highway system, modern corporations, the skyscrapers of our cities, and quietly go on with their lives. I knew one of those men—Col. Carroll Smith. He (then Captain Smith) stepped off a Higgins boat onto Utah Beach with his 29th Infantry Division on D-Day. He pushed, cajoled and dragged his men off the beach then led them as they fought their way up the cliffs to overrun the German positions and secure the bloody beachhead. With very little rest and no time to celebrate their historic victory, the 29th turned to face the German counteroffensive across the rugged and deadly Norman hedgerow country. They fought, sometimes hand-to-hand, to drive the Germans back across the French border and into the heart of the quickly-failing Third Reich. After the war, Col. Smith came home to Albemarle County, Virginia and took up farming. He was proud to have served—he was never without his D-Day lapel pin and was the official leader of the Pledge of Allegiance for our organization. He drove an understated old, rusted station wagon and wore seersucker suits and straw hats around town. He got together with his 29th Division buddies to chew the fat as often as he could, but, as long as I knew him he never once called himself a hero. Never once did he tell tall tales about his fighting prowess or brag about how many Germans he killed. He was just a soldier. Even when I tricked him into telling me stories of the battles (he is profiled in Cornelius Ryan's best-selling book *The Longest Day*) not once did he make himself seem anything other than a young man stuck in the middle of a war doing what he could to survive. He remarked once, after he and fellow D-Day comrades reviewed a local release of the movie *Saving Private Ryan,* "We were just scared boys doing our jobs." These simple leaders do not talk about being leaders—they just lead.

Fred Selfe led.

He led selflessly and with great humility as if he knew the footprints he left to be deep and lasting—he was careful not to do harm as he walked through life. He was the quintessence of the Confucian thought, "Humility is the foundation of all virtues."

As Badaracco states, quiet leaders like Carroll Smith, Bill Crawford and Fred Selfe, "move and change the world." They move and act in and around us without fanfare or celebrity; most times without thanks or recognition. They quietly lead us where we should be going—to greatness.

Muddy Boots Leadership

Before the invasion of Iraq in 2003, Saddam Hussein was criticized as a weak leader out of touch with his own military. Seeking to discredit the dictator, Col. Stuart Herrington, a retired Army counterintelligence officer, reported in a *Washington Post* editorial that one U.S. General claimed, "Saddam never wore *muddy boots.* The man had no training or skills as a soldier."

"Muddy boots" is a military term used to describe officers who go into battle with their men. The term *muddy boots* refers to getting dirty—down in the mud with everyone else; a superior getting their highly shined boots messy from actual toil. These *muddy boots* officers put themselves in harms way—just like the men they command.

Using the term *muddy boots* to describe someone says the leader is respected because they *do* instead of just telling others to do. They come from the back to stand in the front line of battle. They get out of the bunker and go where the action is. They get off their horses and into the field. *Muddy boots* leaders don't ask anyone to do anything they wouldn't do.

Muddy boots leaders are leaders who work alongside their charges to get things done. In an article entitled *Leading in Times of Uncertainty*, Dr. John C. Maxwell tells that Rudolph Giuliani, while mayor of New York during the hours and days following the 9/11 attacks, never stopped working in and around *ground zero*. "Giuliani left the TV on through the night in case the terrorists struck again. He parked his muddy boots next to the bed in case he needed to head out fast."

Sir Ernest Henry Shackleton led an ill-fated 1914 expedition to trek 2,000 miles across the continent of Antarctica. But, before they could set foot on the continent Shackelford's ship, *Endurance*, became stuck in the polar ice. They were dragged for 11 long months before the ship was crushed forcing the crew to abandon her. The entire crew of 28 men and 68 dogs were stranded on an iceberg with no way to leave or contact the outside world.

As leader of the group, Shackleton faced the unenviable task of keeping up morale and keeping his men alive in the sub-zero temperatures and hazards of the uncharted continent. He immediately set assigned work details on a schedule that rotated chores among all the men—including Shackleton. He knew to survive the dangers they must all work together with as little friction and negativity as possible. He quickly dropped the normal chain of command and substituted one of equality among the group. Captain, sailor, and researcher suddenly became men equally at risk, sharing in the dangers and the work. Shackleton even stepped aside when necessary to let other men lead.

After five months living on the ice, Shackleton and five others set sail in a small boat to search for help leaving the majority of the crew behind. They returned three-and-a-half months later to rescue the remaining 22 crew members. Shackleton's muddy boots leadership, or frozen boots leadership in his case, helped the crew of the aptly named *Endurance* survive and return home after more than 16 months of suffering off the coast of Antarctica. Thanks to Shackleton's courageous leadership there were zero casualties during the entire disastrous event.

Fred Selfe was the epitome of the muddy boots leader. As Mike Griffith pointed out, "He would have made a great head coach, at any level, but he was not a political man." Fred Selfe was smart and strong enough to be a head football coach at any school anywhere, but instead chose to remain an assistant coach. He chose to be a quiet leader.

Coach Selfe got involved in his practices, stepped in to show a guard how to block or an end a short route. He was at practice each day long before the players and stayed long after they left for home. He never asked anyone to do anything he would not do himself. In fact, if there was a job or a chore to be done, he would roll up his sleeves and do it. Bob Johnson, a muddy boots leader himself, says of Fred Selfe, "Right now we've got to figure out how to do all the things he did so we can continue to function. The guy did the work of three or four people." I get an eerie feeling now walking around the King Center—his spirit is there but he is not. I cannot remember a time before he died that I could not find him there in *his* building. I say *his* because he cared for it, kept it up and spent most of his time in it. His actual office was a small ten-by-ten cramped space, but I always think of the King Athletic Center as *his*. He cared about it. Sure there was a staff assigned to its upkeep, but he felt it his duty to do the work.

He dressed like his players in blue shorts, gray t-shirts and baseball caps. He walked onto the field with them. He was on the practice field before they got there and stayed long after they left for home. He stood in the huddle with them and he sometimes got down in a three-point stance in the line to show them how to do it *Fred Selfe style*. No one who ever played for Fred Selfe doubted his dedication to his teams or his willingness to work or fight for it. His boots were always muddy.

Servant Leadership

Max Dupree, former CEO and Chairman of the Herman Miller Corporation, a Fortune 500 company, relates this story in his book *Leadership Jazz*: "I arrived at the local tennis club just after a group of high school students had vacated the locker room. Like chickens, they had not bothered to pick up after themselves. Without thinking too much about it, I gathered up all their towels and put them in a hamper. A friend of mine quietly watched me do this and then asked me a question that I've pondered many times over the years. "Do you pick up towels because you're the president of a company, or are you the president because you pick up towels?"

Norm Brodsky, entrepreneur and one of my favorite *Inc.* magazine contributors, tells of getting on a JetBlue fight and while buckling his lap belt noticing a "middle-aged man with slightly graying hair" standing up in front of the plane. "Hi," the man announced, "my name is Dave Neeleman, and I'm the CEO of JetBlue. I'm here to serve you this evening, and I'm looking forward to meeting each of you before we land." Sure enough the CEO of a billion dollar company gave out snacks and sat talking with passengers throughout the flight. Brodsky discovered he does it all the time. Neeleman says it gives him an opportunity to get to know the people who pay the bills.

Servant leadership is an interesting concept that turns the traditional leadership model on its head. Its earliest evangelist, Robert K. Greenleaf, says it "begins with a natural feeling that one wants to serve, to serve first. Then conscious choice brings one to aspire to lead." Greenleaf based his beliefs on his 35 years of experience with AT&T and study of philosophy. "I believe that caring for persons—the more able and the less able serving each other—is what makes a good society."

Servant leadership is not so much a style of management as an attitude of the heart and soul. Danah Zohar, in her book *Re-wiring the Corporate Brain*, goes so far as claiming, "Servant leadership is the essence of quantum thinking and quantum leadership."

Jesus is the ideal example of an effective servant-leader and His actions, indeed, may be considered "quantum." From very early in His ministry He extolled the importance of serving others with humility. In Luke 14: 7-14 He says, "For everyone who exalts himself will be humbled, and he who humbles himself will be exalted."

Jesus taught the universal significance of service to others and offered himself as the ultimate example. In Mark 10: 35-45 He says, "For even the Son of Man did not come to be served, but to *serve*..."

At the end of His time on earth, on the last evening when He had His disciples gathered around Him, He arose from supper and took off His outer garments. Next He took a towel, wrapped it around His waist and poured water into a basin. Then, to the astonishment of His followers, began washing their feet. Simon Peter said to Him, "Lord, do you wash my feet?" Jesus answered him, "You don't know what I am doing now, but you will understand later."

Peter, the rock on which Jesus said he would build his church, said with righteous indignation, "You will never wash my feet!" Jesus answered him, "If I don't wash you, you have no part with me.'

According to The Gospel of John Chapter 13, "So when He had washed their feet, put His outer garment back on, and sat down again, He said to them, *"Do you know what I have done to you? You call me, 'Teacher' and 'Lord.' You say so correctly, for so I am. If I then, the Lord and the Teacher, have washed your feet, you also ought to wash one another's feet. For I have given you an example, that you also should do as I have done to you. Most certainly I tell you, a servant is not greater than his lord, neither one who is sent greater than he who sent him. If you know these things, blessed are you if you do them."*

Even the 12 men closest to Jesus, those who had followed Jesus from the beginning of his quiet ministry in the backwater town of Galilee to His triumphal entry into Jerusalem and to that last supper—even they had trouble understanding why the Christ would squat on a cold stone floor and wash the dirty and mud from their feet. But Jesus made it easy for them to see that the lesson He needed them to learn—the very example of their teacher— was to go out into the world and serve others. It took His resurrection to make them truly believe, but the lesson took root. It grew and the tiny, devout sect of followers of the Christ spread from that small room to every corner of our globe.

Fred Selfe served others. Dr. Robert Russell met Fred Selfe when he refereed Russell's high school wrestling matches. Russell went on to earn an M.B.A., PhD., and join the faculty at Emory and Henry. He says Fred Selfe became a friend, colleague and tough racquetball opponent. Russell writes in a letter to Fred Selfe before his death, "I have always known that if there was any one person I could depend on for help it is you. Almost everyone who has been at Emory and Henry any length of time has known that the best servant on the campus is Fred Selfe. Your *'gosh dandy bullfrog'* approach to life has blessed the souls of hundreds of people."

As you have read in the preceding chapters of this book, he worked and served others without any desire for reward or acknowledgement. Charlie Quillen, Emory and Henry's Senior Development Officer and 1970 graduate of the college, knew Fred Selfe as a friend and fellow college staff member. Quillen describes Fred Selfe in Carter Moore's *EHC Wired* article: "Someone talked about Fred Selfe being selfless, and I think that there are too few selfless individuals in the world. There are too many people getting enamored with decisions, or money or fame. I'll tell you, the people that have those things, in our lifetime, aren't going to affect positively nearly the number of people that people like Fred Selfe will. Lots of people have gotten honors or fame or glory in their lifetime, but Fred Selfe did none of those; he was humility personified."

Bob Johnson's father, Gen. Harold K. Johnson served as Chief of Staff of the Army from 1964-1968 at the height of America's involvement in the war in Vietnam and appeared on the cover of *Time* magazine as one of the most influential people of his time. Bob Johnson served as a Ranger platoon leader in the 101st Airborne in that war and has recorded more than 300 wins as head basketball coach at Emory and Henry. His own leadership is honored in a recent television documentary, *From Ballfields to Battlefields*. I believe his experiences in the military, in war, and as a record-setting head basketball coach give him a unique understanding of what makes good leaders. Johnson says of Fred Selfe, "He knew that leadership is not about getting the good stuff—the big house, the big car, the big money or the adulation. He knew leadership was about *doing* the good stuff."

If Robert Greenleaf and Danah Zohar are correct and servant leadership is "what makes a good society," and the "essence of quantum thinking," then Bob Johnson is right and Fred Selfe is the ideal example for millions of people "doing the good stuff." Johnson adds, "When one attempts to define anything one looks to the finest example from there. The perfect baseball swing: Ted Williams or Henry Aaron. The prefect shooting stroke in basketball: Larry Bird or Michael Jordan. The perfect gold swing: Tiger Woods or Ben Hogan. The life lived quietly and humbly in service to others: *Fred Selfe.*"

SIX GREAT BIG SMALL THINGS

1)   *As Iron Sharpens Iron,* **Your Life Can Sharpen So Many Others**
2)   **Beat Your Wings**
3)   **Be Courageous and Contagious**
4)   **Build a Strong House**
5)   **Put Your Principles Into Action**
6)   **Be a Good, Quiet, Muddy Boots, Servant Leader and LEAD**

LEARN AND USE THE 15 TRIED AND TRUE CHARACTERISTICS OF GOOD LEADERS:

1.   Be Courageous
2.   Live with Integrity
3.   Be Accountable
4.   Sacrifice Your Personal Interests
5.   Be an Optimist
6.   Trust Your Coup D'Oeil
7.   Strive for Excellence Not Perfection
8.   Stay *on Mission*
9.   Serve Others First
10.   Empower Others

11. Have Deep Concern for Others and Treat Them with Respect and Dignity
12. Listen
13. Reward Great Performers
14. Challenge Yourself and Others
15. Keep it Simple

USE ALL THREE LEADERSHIP STYLES. MAKE THEM PART OF YOUR LIFE— THE VERY WAY YOU LIVE EACH DAY.

Lead as a **Quiet Leader** who goes about doing what is right without thoughts of reward or recognition. Be the undercurrent that keeps those around you afloat and moves them toward greatness.

Lead as a **Muddy Boots Leader** who never asks anyone to do what you would not. Get down off your horse and into the trenches to work alongside those you lead. Get your boots dirty to get things done.

Lead as a **Servant Leader** who seeks first to serve others, then naturally aspires to lead. Make the world about others—serve selflessly. Wash the feet of those who follow you. Serve without stopping and teach your followers to serve those who follow them.

SEVENTH GREAT BIG SMALL THING

Teach Others to Teach

When you teach your son, you teach your son's son.
The Talmud

Good leaders are good teachers and good teachers are good because they teach others to teach. That is a mouthful! It will never sell many bumper-stickers, but it is the best way to say it. We all teach—whether it is as a teacher within our educational system, coach of a sports team, manager of a company, member of a family, church or synagogue, in an elected position, or just living in a neighborhood. Our social interconnectedness puts us squarely in the position of constantly teaching others around us and we become good teachers as we teach others to teach.

My first boss was a leader-teacher. John Ginn, father of my friend and fellow Richlands High Tornado and E&H *Wasp*, Jack Ginn (the first head football coach at North Carolina Wesleyan College in Rocky Mount) gave me my first job at his company in Anderson, South Carolina. John was publisher and president of a large media company made up of a daily newspaper, a commercial printing division, a newsletter company, a number of shopping guides and supplemental publications, and a small advertising agency for which I became the lone copywriter. He was a tall, salty-bearded, barrel-chested man with a booming voice and a big, generous laugh. He was a brilliant, hard-working man who headed a company of 400 people doing many different jobs and doing them well. I remember John stepping into my tiny windowless office hidden away in the corner of the huge building almost every day to say hello and ask how things were going. He popped in some days and flashed tickets to a Clemson University basketball or football game and asked what time he should pick me up. During our ride to the Clemson campus he talked about things I was encountering in my new life in the world of business—the loss of a colleague to cancer, buying my first real car, learning to work as a team with highly creative people, working across divisions with different goals and deadlines. I remember John letting me talk about these things and asking question after question sparking more discussion and more questions. By the time he dropped me off after the game I felt I got not only free tickets to a sports event, but a free lesson toward my MBA. The lessons were simple and straight-forward, so when I got together with friends who were starting out in their first jobs we could discuss the same issues and I could pass John Ginn's thoughts on to them. I still use them in managing people almost 17 years later. John Ginn was a good leader because he was a good teacher and a good teacher because he taught others to teach.

As I am a Christian, I will use another Biblical story to illustrate this point. The relationship between Moses and Joshua shows how important teaching others to teach is. Moses was the great leader who led the Israelites out of bondage in Egypt and toward the *Promised Land*. Joshua was chosen from the ranks of battlefield commanders to attend Moses. He became Moses' apprentice and stayed in that position for 40 long years as they wandered in the wilderness. He was known as "Moses' assistant" and "his servant" in Exodus 24:13; 33:11. That may seem like a long time—especially in our microwave world where taking a minute to launch your computer's browser is an eternity—but Joshua was tasked by God to serve Moses and serve he did. Moses knew Joshua would inherit his role as leader, so he spent the time teaching Joshua to lead. He studied Joshua to learn the skills he needed to develop then *situationally* taught Joshua those skills. Moses was mentored by his father-in-law Jethro. After the escape from Egypt, Moses found himself leader, sole judge, and chief question answerer for the entire Jewish flock. Finally, in Exodus 18:14 Jethro asks him, *"What is this thing you do to the people?"* Moses thought he was protecting the people, but he was limiting them. So, Jethro convinced Moses to create an administrative system of judges and mid-level managers so help lead and serve the people as they wandered. His leadership flourished. Moses, in turn, mentored Joshua who studied how Moses handled the rebellion of the Israelites, trusted God to perform miracles like parting the Red Sea, supply bread from heaven, and crack open a rock to give water. He saw how Moses spent time alone with God in prayer, how he interceded for the people, and how he delegated responsibility to others. Each incident gave Joshua a chance to learn to lead. Joshua was only the second person to lead the Israelites in their early turbulent history. He took the mantle from Moses to lead them into the land of Canaan where God had declared Moses would not enter. Following a great leader is usually difficult and usually does not lend itself to individual greatness. Who remembers the man who spoke *after* Lincoln delivered his Gettysburg Address or the second man on the moon? As fullbacks, Richie Hooker and I ran the ball only once in every 10 or so plays, our function was to block for Sandy Rogers and Gary Collier so they could score touchdowns and set NCAA records. Joshua, however, shone brightly as the new leader of the Israelites. He spent so many years learning from Moses that he was able to lead in a time of great change. In fact, Joshua is considered one of the most competent leaders in the history of the Jewish people and not until hundreds of years later does a comparable leader, Samuel, appear.

Fred Selfe knew he was training teachers and coaches. He knew many of the young people around him would leave Emory and Henry to become high school teachers, college professors or join football and baseball coaching staffs around the country. He understood and accepted this responsibility and he made sure he did the right things to help them become leaders. Like Chris Musser's story in which Fred Selfe advises the young coach, *"Prepare them as well as you can and let them play."* He was teaching Chris to teach the players Chris would encounter in his coming years as a coach.

Some of his players ended up on the opposite side of the field coaching against their alma mater. Temple Musser tells a story of returning to Emory and Henry as an assistant football coach for ODAC rival Randolph-Macon College: "I was dreading it because we had to come down here . . . I was dreading it all season because I knew I had to meet that man. He was my hero; he was my mentor . . . my coach the year before. I didn't know how he felt about that . . . going head to head. I was coming across the field and I get to about mid-field or so, and there he is standing on the sidelines— hands on his hips, and he is giving me *the look*. He is staring me down. I probably start getting to the hash mark and I see this little grin start forming and obviously it helped me make those last few steps. You know, I thought it would be a handshake, but by the time I got to the sideline he was waiting on me and gave me great big hug. That is my most cherished moment . . . with Coach Selfe, because at that moment I realized he is proud of me—win or lose, it didn't matter. He was there to win a football game, and I had come down to do the same."

Bridges

Emory and Henry College is known for training educators. At the college's 2004 annual Forum on Education, former Virginia Governor Gerald Baliles congratulated the college on that legacy and spoke about the need to continue teaching people to teach: "In the rural areas where agriculture has long been a way of life, citizens instantly understand that one reaps what one sows." He continues, "If the seeds of education are not sown throughout the areas for all its citizens, then where is the harvest and where is the future?" Fred Selfe knew this. His education in Castlewood, where the entire high school enrollment was around 300 people, gave him the opportunity to learn and go on to Virginia Tech then Emory and Henry. His work there gave him the tools to go on to ETSU for his master's degree.

Growing up in the small, rural, coal-mining and farming town of Richlands, Virginia, I relate to Fred Selfe's upbringing and testify living in a rural area gives one a unique respect for educators. Education is the key to doing and being more than what you see around you. It is the only way (other than joining the military—which many young men and women do) to move beyond that small town or community to see and experience the world. Richlands is a wonderful place. I go back there as often as I can to see the natural beauty and the people I grew up among. One of my favorite things in the world is to go to church there on Sunday morning. I look forward to going into that tall-raftered chapel and being greeted by familiar faces, or gathering outside the entrance after the service to be kissed on the cheek by women who used to play bridge with my grandmother or attend the Garden Club with my mother. It reminds me of my childhood and all the wonders I discovered there. However, once I grew up and attended high school the only options to stay in the town were to work in the coal mines, or find some other job that might pay minimum wage, but add little value to my existence. I wanted more. My grandmother, Louise Graham McGlothlin—a teacher by profession—spent hours with me on the floor of her house flipping through encyclopedias pushing me to discover what was out in the big world. We started with A and page after page, entry after entry, month after month worked our way through Z. Because of her influence, I worked hard to get into college so I could see some of the things I saw on those pages. And I had lots of help from teachers and school administrators.

In my small hometown teachers are granted a respect approaching the kind usually reserved for professionals—doctors, lawyers, dentists. They are bridges—ways out and across—for people who want more.

This appreciation is not confined to rural areas. My great friend Paul C. Harris grew up in the inner city of Charlottesville and feels the same. Paul spent his childhood in a low income government subsidized housing project. He never knew his father, and his young mother, Pauline, worked as many as three jobs to keep them fed and clothed. It was not easy, in fact, Paul says it was downright difficult and sometimes looked impossible to a small boy with clothes he called "third and fourth-hand." But Pauline kept a smile on her face and told Paul over and over he should not curse the darkness, but "light a candle." She pushed him to learn, do his homework and his best in school. She understood Paul's *candle* was education. Teacher's recognized Paul's eagerness and devotion to learning and went out of their way to give him the tools he needed. With his mother's guidance and his teachers' dedication he worked harder and received an academic scholarship to attend the Miller School, a military-style boarding school in Albemarle County. Pauline even sold her car—took the bus to her three jobs—to pay for his books. She made a sweat and tears equity investment in her son's future.

Paul excelled at Miller School and went on to attend Hampton University, where, again he worked hard to stay in the top percentage of his class. Next he put himself through the George Washington University School of Law while working fulltime.

All those years of hard work and attention to education paid off for the boy from the housing projects: He went to work for the largest law firm in Virginia, became the first black Republican elected to the Virginia General Assembly since 1891, chosen by the Bush Administration as Deputy Assistant U.S. Attorney General, and is now Senior Counsel for the mega-company Raytheon. He has a beautiful wife, Monica—a teacher—and three wonderful children. Paul's candle burns brighter than ever—thanks to a mother who knew the value of a good education and teachers who taught and cared for their students.

Gosh Dandy, Bullfrog!

Fred Selfe recognized the role he played as an educator and role model. He took it very seriously. I never heard him curse—sure he lost his temper once in awhile—he was human no matter how superhuman he seemed—but I never heard a true curse word come from his mouth. Nonsensical words and phrases like *"Gosh dandy!"* and *"Bullfrog!"* were the worst you might hear. Another of my favorites was *"Horsefeathers!"* These hallmark sayings did the job. If you heard one with a stern tone attached you knew something had gone terribly wrong and it was better to stand very still in case it was you.

He knew he had to retain the respect of his players and students, so he did his absolute best to *do his absolute best.* Bruce Hatch agrees, "I think deep down inside he knew—and from very early in his coaching career—he knew the part he was playing in people's lives. And, I think that shaped his character—shaped the way that he went about his job everyday, because he knew he was having an influence on people."

Warren Buffet, the Oracle of Omaha, holds an annual meeting of Berkshire Hathaway—the amazingly successful company he has been running since 1965—shareholders in the company's hometown of Omaha, Nebraska. Close to 20,000 people pack the room to hear and meet Buffet. They want him as their mentor, and Buffet is happy to oblige. At the April, 2004 meeting Buffet spent nearly six hours fielding questions from the attendees. In a recent *Money* magazine article, writer Jason Zweig quotes Buffet as saying, "Even though Ben Graham [Buffet's mentor] had everything he needed in life, he still wanted to give something back by teaching . . . so, just as we got it from somebody else, we don't want it to stop with us. We want to pass it along too."

Mentoring others to mentor—teaching others to teach—is something anyone can do. First, you must accept the responsibility of being a teacher then go about doing it. Fred Selfe trained perhaps 1,000 coaches and teachers in his career. He taught them to accept the same responsibility of teaching, attain and keep respect, and to teach others to do the same. He created an action chain that, as I mention over and over, continues to grow into the storm worthy of Lorenz's *butterfly effect.*

SEVEN GREAT BIG SMALL THINGS

1) *As Iron Sharpens Iron*, Your Life Can Sharpen So Many Others
2) Beat Your Wings
3) Be Courageous and Contagious
4) Build a Strong House
5) Put Your Principles Into Action
6) Be a Good, Quiet, Muddy Boots, Servant Leader and LEAD
7) Teach Others to Teach

How many people have you influenced with your life? How many people have you taught? How many people have you taught to teach others?

Surround yourself with people who teach you and whom you can teach. According to the Jason Zweig's *Money* magazine article, when asked by a 14-year-old how to succeed in life, Warren buffet quipped, "Hang out with people whose behavior is better than yours, and then you'll drift in the right direction."

Teach others to teach, for as my friend Paul Harris' mother knew, "To light a candle is to cast a shadow." Fred Selfe, as Bruce Hatch points out, "Enjoyed talking about his former players. He enjoyed talking about their careers, their accomplishments, and their families." He taught them to teach others—they did, so his life expanded through them. It still does.

Teach others to teach.

EIGHTH GREAT BIG SMALL THING

The Four F Words: Forgive, Forget, Focus, Forward

If all you have is a hammer, everything looks like a nail.

Anonymous

The beatings will continue until morale improves. That is one of my favorite humorous sayings. I laughed out loud when I first read it on a bumper sticker on a small car in Chapel Hill, North Carolina right beside one that read *I used all my sick days, so I'm calling in dead.* Although I do not know the origins of this humorous saying, I imagine it written into a memo at some backward company by a bad manager trying to push people to do more. Newsflash folks—negative reinforcement, of which beatings surely are, achieves very little when it comes to motivating change in behavior of free-thinking, emotional animals. Pushing gets you nowhere—leading from the front works better and it certainly improves the view.

This amusing little saying about morale encapsulates the leadership style of many really bad leaders. Ever had a boss who yelled at you to get something done? Did you *want* to do it? Did doing the task bring you any fulfillment? Did you do it with heart? I'll bet you answered no to all of those, because morale is never improved by the use of fear. Good leaders know how to treat those they want to follow them. Beatings—physical or verbal—are not the way.

Fred Selfe understood this. He respected his players and students. He understood their mistakes were his mistakes too. He led from the front. He walked in the direction he thought the right way and people followed. He was a shepherd who walked toward sustenance and safety—in the right direction—and led only those *wanted* to follow him.

One of his greatest attributes—the one that rounds out the *Selfe Factor*—was his ability to forgive. He understood nothing is gained from holding onto anger or being punitive.

Joe-Joe Collins tells a story that illustrates how Fred Selfe handled mistakes. Collins and some fellow dormitory suitemates decided to host a small party to mark the end of two-a-day practices when football players move out of the cramped, freshman dorm, Hillman Hall and into their own dorms. As Emory and Henry is a small school, word of the party quickly spread and soon got way out of hand. Both floors of Stuart Hall were filled with football players who had been cooped up on campus for the past two weeks, lots of new students—mostly female—loud music and cold beer. It was a recipe for certain calamity. "The next day, word got back to us we had been found out and our names turned in to campus authorities. Since the entire football team was there, the situation looked grim. To make it worse, since it started in my room, I was listed as a 'ring leader'. The thought of my parents finding out was extremely troubling, but when I thought I might have to face Coach Selfe, I became physically sick at my stomach. I told myself *maybe he doesn't know, yet* when we walked onto the practice field the following day. As I made my way onto the field, feeling like a convicted felon, I spotted him removing equipment from the storage shed. Unfortunately, I had to go right by that shed to get to my starting post for the pre-practice run. I put on my helmet thinking somehow it might make me invisible. As I got closer to the storage shed, I carefully glanced over in his direction to find him staring right through me. I went from a walk to a jog. Suddenly, I felt a steel clamp on my shoulder that halted my progress mid-stride. I turned to find Coach Selfe peering over his tinted glasses. He asked in a voice I didn't recognize, '*Is what I heard about you true?*' His grip got tighter and my legs went limp. I could barely speak, but managed to utter, 'What . . . what do you mean?' He simply repeated his original question. So help me, I couldn't answer him. I just stood there in silence feeling small. I felt more ashamed and upset with myself than I'd ever been. I could see in his face I had let him down and that made me feel about as low as I could. He shook me back and forth a few times and said *'You're better than that, Mr. Collins—make it right'*. He then let me go and turned to get back to work. I realized later he was not concerned I let him down—what he cared about was that I let myself down. After that, I worked harder to do better in football and as a student; I wanted to be the best I could be. I did not want to let anyone down, especially myself. His care and concern made all the difference in how I have lived my life since."

We were playing our arch-rivals Hampden-Sydney College one year in Farmville. It was an unseasonably hot autumn day and we were really battling it out with the Tigers in their vintage stadium. Other than Washington and Lee University, this was probably our most anticipated game, so we were fighting for every inch. On a play called *31 Speed* I was supposed to take off at a sprint around the end leading the running back up the field. My main job was to take out the cornerback—which, oddly enough, Hampden-Sydney trained to squat in one place as I barreled down on him with a 15-yard charging head start. Gary Collier called the play in the huddle, we lined up and off we went. I could feel the tailback, Sandy Rogers (who broke the NCAA national rushing record that year with 1,730 single season yards) breathing down my neck as we turned the corner. I looked back for a brief second for some reason then up the field again to find no cornerback. I looked left then right and kept on going up the field until I heard the whistle blow the play over. I came to a stop and looked back to find Sandy and Gary in a pile with one lone Tiger—that darned cornerback. When I looked back—which is a *no-no* in a speed offense—he shot up field and stopped the play. Richie Hooker came in from the sidelines to take my place. I jogged off the field with my head down, slipped in beside Coach Selfe and waited for an earful. Nothing happened. Two plays later he grabbed my shoulder pads and stuck his face right down against my facemask. "You think you can find that cornerback this time?" He asked in a low, smoldering voice.

"Yes sir!" I shot back eager to make him proud. "I guarantee I can find him if you give me another chance."

"Get it done," he said with a wry smile. Then he gave me a good shove and off I went me to the huddle. Gary called *31 Speed* and this time I would have moved heaven and earth to knock that guy down. I did. In fact, I think I hit the guy so hard we ended up way off the sidelines and Sandy got a big first down. I remember Sunday evening when that play came up on the game film, Coach Selfe re-ran it three or four times because the hit was so explosive—and I think to remind me there was a wrong way and a right way to run *31 Speed*.

When people disappointed Fred Selfe, he did not rant or rave he just wanted you to "make it right." He wanted you to get it done. Fred Selfe knew being right is never more important than getting the job done. He could have preached a long sermon to Joe-Joe Collins on the wrongs of the party. He could have taken me out of the game, lit into me about missing a block and left me on the sidelines, but that was not his style of leadership. He knew *we knew* we made mistakes and he let us know all he wanted was for us to "make it right."

If God Didn't Forgive, Heaven Would Be Empty

That is the kind of forgiveness good leaders and strong people exhibit. Being angry with someone is easy—it is a base human emotion. You do not have to think to be mad. Someone steals your girlfriend or boyfriend, takes advantage of your kindness or slights you in some way anger is the first thing that pops up. It is just there. Forgiveness, on the other hand, is difficult because it requires a higher level of thinking. You have to push past the first emotion to get refocused on the bigger picture. If your team is working for a first down, or trying to protect a lead by running down the clock and one of your players makes a mistake, you cannot let that take you *off mission*. As I said in the chapter on leadership, one of the most important traits of good leadership is keeping people *on mission*—focused on the bigger job at hand. You must stay focused AND you must keep those following you focused. Throughout my career in management I have heard people moan about why they are not head of the department or a manager. When they get their chance, though, they often forget with the increase in pay or new title come increased responsibilities. When you are the leader *you* are sailing the ship. When you hit rough waters the crew looks to *you* for the solution and protection. It is a responsibility one should never take lightly and accept it only when you are ready to put the mission first and yourself second.

If your goal is to throw your power and position around to impress people, teaching and coaching are not for you. In fact, managing and leading anything—other than maybe a pack of poodles—is not for you. I think psychologists will tell you if you need to impose your power on people so they fear you, you have some deeper problems that stem from how you feel about yourself.

Leadership is not about getting the glory—it is about getting things done. Fred Selfe is one the finest examples of this maxim. He used a simple technique I teach my managers: Fix the problem not the blame.

Fred Selfe held sway over the entire offense—50 young men. He had the power to do anything he wanted. Punish, release from the team, or apply any punitive measures he wished. His advanced leadership style, though, was to see the entire picture, react quickly and solve problems with the bigger goal—the mission—in mind.

When we all sat together as an offense to go over the game film he would pause on mistakes. He would rerun the film once if it was as simple mistake; twice if it was a really bad mistake then move on. He knew there was no need to push the point. Players were embarrassed by their mistakes because they knew it had cost the team in some way and that was punishment enough.

EIGHT GREAT BIG SMALL THINGS

1)   **As *Iron Sharpens Iron*, Your Life Can Sharpen So Many Others**
2)   **Beat Your Wings**
3)   **Be Courageous and Contagious**
4)   **Build a Strong House**
5)   **Put Your Principles Into Action**
6)   **Be a Good, Quiet, Muddy Boots, Servant Leader and LEAD**
7)   **Teach Others to Teach**
8)   **Forgive and Forget the Mistakes of Others**

The *Eighth Great Big Small Thing* is rerun the film then move on. Do not get caught up in the pettiness of holding grudges or using your power over others as a weapon. Use your power as a leader to serve others and stay *on mission* to achieving your goals.

Forgive and forget the mistakes of others; focus on the goal and move forward.

NINTH
GREAT BIG
SMALL THING

The *Selfe Factor*:
The Incremental Revolution

*Your 'gosh dandy bullfrog' approach to life has
blessed the souls of hundreds of people.*
Dr. Robert Russell

I have a friend who refuses to use recipes when she cooks
a meal. Which is not necessarily a bad thing, but she also
has ADD—Attention Deficit Disorder—so you really never
know how anything she makes is going to taste. There is
no constancy to her dishes because she cannot stay
focused on the task at hand. Sometimes her meals are
good and sometimes inedible. She once made a sauce for
some fresh dolphin I brought over and it was great. The
next time I brought over fresh tuna she made a different

sauce that ruined the tuna. I swear I think it had maple syrup in it. Recipes can be good things—they give you tried and true models for cooking. Of course you can add your own flair and substitute one thing for another, as long as it is complimentary to the original ingredient. I would not suggest you swap maple syrup for anything in a fish sauce recipe, but you can make some simple changes as long as it jibes with the overall makeup of things. Throwing in a pinch of freshly grated nutmeg to a cream sauce will enhance the flavor—lemon will curdle and ruin it.

The *Selfe Factor* is something of a recipe for making yourself into a better person. Each virtue, or *small thing*, is an ingredient that mixes to make a Great Big Thing for your betterment and the progress of those around you. Following the recipe is highly suggested—after all, these are the ingredients that made up Fred Sefle, and as you have witnessed, thousands of people consider him one of the best people they ever encountered.

Now we get to how you can use the *Selfe Factor* for changing your life into something new and better. As I said before, this change you are about to make is a revolution—it is a momentous change in *who* and *what* you are. However, the *Selfe Factor* is made up the *Great Big Small Things* that help you carry out a revolution in steps—an incremental revolution—carried out one day at a time. Let's say you want to change yourself 100 percent over the next year, you can use each of the *Great Big Small Things* to do it. The theory behind the incremental revolution is you can completely change yourself by changing just three tenths of one percent—.3 percent each day. Do something—anything—that amounts to a tiny .3 percent each day and at the end of the year you will have changed 100 percent and been able to take a few days off! *Great Big Small Things* are the daily .3 percent that guarantees the success of your incremental revolution. Remember Coach Lou Holtz's advice: "You build a successful life one day at a time."

As the *Fifth Great Big Small Thing* points out, knowing these things without putting them into action is useless. So, I suggest you go with the flow here and do them one step—one glorious day at a time.

Step 1)   Recognize you need the *small thing* in your life

If you are contemplating personal courage, look around and notice the hypocrisy, mediocrity and apathy in your life and the world. Did you vote in the most recent election? Did you stand up to someone who took advantage of you? Did you visit that elderly friend in the hospital? Did you shovel the snow from a sick neighbor's driveway? If you answered *no* to these questions, realize that is certainly not the way it is supposed to be. Look, and really see, what you've been looking away from: the dishonesty, disrespect, irresponsibility, lack of compassion, and unfair things and people around you. Once you see these things you can take the next step and do something about them. Take Danny Carter's advice,

"Make every day count, appreciate every moment and take from it everything that you possibly can, for you may never be able to experience it again. Hold your head up because you have every right to. Create your own life and then go out and live it."

Step 2)   Think of Fred Selfe and act

See where personal courage may be applied and apply it. "Get it done!" as Fred Selfe would say. Put what you've learned into action. Stop putting it off and do it. A map is no good unless you are driving a car—a plan is nothing until you put it into action. My mother learned she had Multiple Sclerosis in the early 1970s and sat and cried for days. Once she was through the grief stage, she got up and went to work. She sat on the phone for hours counseling others she met with M.S.; poured through medical journals and articles about possible cures, and talked to anyone she thought might help. When the disabling effects began she lost her equilibrium and the use of her legs—but she did not sit in bed for long. She got right to work getting into a clinical drug trial and spent many grueling hours over many months learning to walk again. She refused to sit and think about the disease—she acted to make things better. It worked. She has been in remission since the late 1970s, continues to counsel others and searches for a permanent cure for the disease.

Step 3)   Make it a habit

Like any new thing, you must repeat it and use it in order to keep it. "The second half of a man's life," says Fyodor Dostoevsky, "is made up of nothing but the habits he has acquired during the first half." Use the *small thing* each day in some way. Suddenly, you will use it without thinking and surprise yourself. Once it is a habit, it is part of who you are—it is your character. If your incremental revolution is to succeed you must do the .3 percent each and every day. If that .3 percent is a habit, it happens when you are not looking and, like the tiny butterfly wings, changes your complex system—your life.

Step 4)   Use the small things to lead others

Wherever you find yourself involved—your family, church, coaching a team, teaching, managing, as part of a team, in your neighborhood and community—choose to lead. Stand up with your courage and start moving in the right direction. People will follow. Once you know and accept the *15 tried and true characteristics of good leaders,* put on the *three styles of leadership*, and study the examples of Fred Selfe's leadership, you will find you must step up and lead. Use what you know—we need you. Become a quiet, muddy boots and servant leader and watch the world change beneath your feet.

Step 5)   Teach what you know to others so they may teach it to others

Again, not the catchiest of bumper stickers, but it is the key to proving the First Law of Thermodynamics—that Fred Selfe's life continues through you and those you teach these *small things*. What would it be like to have the majority of the world's population experiencing *great big things* in their lives? How would that change the picture? It all begins with you.   Know that as the Talmud says, "When you teach your son, you teach your son's son."

Step 6)   Accept there will be mistakes

Yours and those you lead—along the way. Embrace mistakes and learn from them. Re-run the film to take a look at what went wrong then move on. Keep *on mission* and keep those around you *on mission*. The *small things* only work if you are working on a great big thing. Do not stall your revolution because of your own ego or insecurities—keep it moving forward. Forgive, forget, focus, forward. Always forward.

Step 7)   Persevere

Keep on keeping on. The front side of Virginia's State Seal is well known: the Roman-garbed goddess *Virtue* standing with her foot planted on the chest of a vanquished despot and the motto *Sic Semper Tyrannis—Thus Always to Tyrants* beneath. The reverse side of the seal is not as well-known, but just as interesting. It features three Roman goddesses, Liberty, Eternity and

Fruitfulness, and the motto *Perservando—by Persevering*. Only through persevering—sticking to your guns, doing these small things each and every day regardless of what obstacles or challenges get in your way—can you achieve lasting freedom and prosperity. Coach Selfe did small things regardless of what others did or thought, regardless of what his peers may have advised, regardless of the difficulty or sacrifice it required because he believed it to be his lot in life. Keep on keeping on. Others may think you too short or missing some qualifications; if you want something work each day to achieve it. Be like the five–foot-tall basketball standout, Bronie Reynolds, believe in yourself and work to be what *you* want.

Step 8)   Honor heroes

People like Fred Selfe are all around us. You probably know one or two, but maybe just consider them *good people*. You may not call them heroes because you think of that title in mythical terms—Achilles, King Arthur, William Wallace, Davy Crockett, Robert E, Lee, or Winston Churchill.

Heroes—the real kind—are people who sacrifice their own comfort to help others: The mother who quits her job to raise a child; the teacher who reaches into her own pocket to buy supplies to fully educate her students; the volunteer who delivers food to the poor and disabled; the coach who goes out of the way to care for and teach his players. Fred Selfe was a hero to thousands who knew him—people who saw his courage, strong character, perseverance, kindness and caring. He did not *practice random acts of kindness* instead he practiced *deliberate acts of kindness*. He made it a habit to help others.

Stop looking for big heroes and see the small ones—the real ones. In fact, be one yourself. As a tavern keeper advised Gilgamesh, the superhero warrior of Mesopotamia in 2800 BC who kept going off in search of his next big conquest and coming back disappointed: "The life you seek you will never find . . . gaze on the child who holds your hand, let your wife enjoy your repeated embrace! For such is the destiny of mortal men." The small things in life make it worth living.

Step 9)   Recognize there are no little things

When legendary singer-songwriter Warren Zevon, of *Werewolves of London* and *Excitable Boy* fame, was in his final days of battling lung cancer David Letterman devoted an entire show to him. Letterman asked Zevon if the cancer had given him any special insight or wisdom. Zevon thought for a moment and replied, "Enjoy every sandwich." Enjoy every small thing. Each second you live you take another breath, but I bet you take that breath for granted. Is that breath a *little thing*? It may seem that way until another one does not come. It then becomes the single most important thing in the world. I heard a story from a visiting minister once about waking up in a hospital to the sound of a loud thumping in his ears. He first thought it the construction he witnessed when he came into the hospital the day before—perhaps the massive pile driver getting the site ready for the foundation of the new wing. The thumping was so loud he prayed for God to make it stop. As he grew more awake he realized the thumping was the beating of the new heart he was in the hospital to have transplanted and quickly changed his prayer asking God to please NOT make it stop. *Small things* only seem small when they stand alone. When you do each of the *small things* in this book together they become, as I mentioned earlier, ingredients going into the recipe for a bigger dish—a new you. Think big—think *Great Big* and you will come to agree with Bruce Barton: "*There are no little things.*"

NINE GREAT BIG SMALL THINGS

1) *As Iron Sharpens Iron*, Your Life Can Sharpen So Many Others
2) Beat Your Wings
3) Be Courageous and Contagious
4) Build a Strong House
5) Put Your Principles Into Action
6) Be a Good, Quiet, Muddy Boots, Servant Leader and LEAD
7) Teach Others to Teach
8) Forgive and Forget the Mistakes of Others
9) Use the Selfe Factor—"Enjoy Every Sandwich"

Fred Selfe lived these things. He did them with ease because somewhere back in his early life he learned them and made them a habit. They became the foundation on which he built his character. I read a "memorable quote" in a recent *Sports Illustrated* magazine by legendary 49ers quarterback, Joe Montana. San Francisco was in the huddle on their own eight yard line with 3:20 left in Super Bowl XXIII trailing the Cincinnati Bengals by less than a touchdown. What words of encouragement and wisdom does Montana give to his anxious teammates in the huddle? "*Isn't that John Candy?*" He spotted the comedian in the stands and wondered aloud if he was correct. His teammates understood. It was what they did time and again—take the ball and drive down the field to score. Montana coolly went on to lead his team 92 yards to win the game 20-16. Even in the most challenging moments, when actions are habits—part of *who* you are—they naturally come to the front. Joe Montana should have—were he a normal human—been scared to near apoplexy; instead his professionalism took over. He looked around Joe Robbie Stadium, got excited about seeing John Candy and led his team the length of the field to win a Super Bowl.

I sincerely hope this book does justice to Fred Selfe and his life. I also hope I have conveyed the lessons he taught and given you good examples of why and how to use them in your own life. I trust it will give you the tools to make the changes that help make your personal incremental revolution successful. I agree with the sentiments of his daughter Paige, "I really need him right now. I need him to help me raise my children. He always knew the answers, had the time, and made the chore fun. He was so creative and smart. I have never met a smarter man. I am scared too . . . he was the person I could talk to about problems . . . financial problems with employees or bosses; problems with my friends, with Mom, my kids or my work performance."

We all need him. This same void Paige is experiencing exists across our culture—it's time for you to step in and fill it.

Bronwyn Reynolds, the college's five-foot-tall former women's basketball standout, issues a wonderful challenge to those who want to be better and search for guidance: "For those of you who never knew Coach Selfe, I hope this will help give you an idea of the kind of man he was. For those of you who played for Coach Selfe, I admire you and all you must have learned. For those of us who did know Coach Selfe, I share this challenge with you: Pass on the lessons we learned from this man to our mediocre world. Lessons learned outside the classroom. Can we go through one day without saying a curse word? Can we pick up a broom and help the custodian sweep the building? Can we motivate a young person to achieve goals with a positive impact, rather than a negative one? Can we respect another person without passing judgment? Can we *be* Fred Selfe?"

Echo with me the aspiration of Josh Wellenhoffer: "As I grow older I want to change and when I change I want to change into Coach Selfe and care for everyone." Be and do *Great Big Small Things* each day and insure your legacy— your *butterfly effect*—creates the same righteous storm Fred Selfe started.

Be Fred Selfe.

EPILOGUE

A CELEBRATION OF LIFE

A Personal Narrative on
The Loss of a Hero

The exit appeared from nowhere. I pushed too hard on the brakes as, suddenly, the big brown sign announcing Emory and Henry College to the right appeared. Cold coffee sloshed over the rim of a Styrofoam cup and onto the console as I snapped out of the fog that had enveloped me since I left Greensboro, North Carolina three hours earlier. I looked out at the dull morning world around me. I noticed the white winter snow that wrapped me like a blanket on my drive, insulating me and my secret thoughts from anything other than a constant white blur, was actually a dusty shade of gray mottled with patches of sodden grass and bare muddy spots.

I also noticed it was cold. I spent the last three hours so deep in my own thoughts of other times and places I neglected to turn on the heat. My fingers were pale and stiff as I peeled them from the steering wheel. I flexed them while I rolled to a stop at the familiar dairy farm at the end of the exit ramp from Interstate 81. They hurt, probably had for an hour or so, but I had not noticed until this moment.

This brought back an immediate memory from days long gone: the heat of the dog days of August during two-a-day football practices and the smell of that dairy farm drifting over the campus; hanging over the practice field until it became hard to breathe the thick, putrid air. That was many years ago. This day I could see my breath and the dairy farm looked deserted.

I turned right through the understated gates of the campus entrance, purposefully passed up the street I should have turned onto and drove on without hesitation. As I crested the hill on which the main gabled and columned administrative building sits overlooking the campus, I saw a dull patchwork quilt of browns, grays, and dirty white stretched out beneath. Facing me was the chapel with its towering wood-shingled spire framed against the ashen sky. I looked away and drove on.

It was not the school I remembered. Although I spent only four years there, and that was more than 15 years ago, it seems to take up three-quarters of my memories and, as my friends and family will attest, almost all the stories I tell about "back in the day." In my mind I see good old Emory and Henry dressed in its finest Blue Ridge highlands autumnal splendor—with flags of blue and bright gold wavering in the crisp air against a background of vibrant yellows, shocking oranges, and the bold, fire-like reds of huge oaks, maples and poplars that shade the campus and give it the small college look that dresses up the front of every marketing piece the college distributes. That day the school looked exactly as I felt— sad.

The college's geographic home, Southwestern Virginia, is an area perhaps best known for being *unknown*. It quietly sits in the extreme western reaches of a state that once stretched to the far side of the unexplored west. Here Virginia's tallest mountains jut up from the neatly cultivated fields like giant dragon's teeth eating the world from within. These mountains that surround the college are the ignored younger sibling of the famous Smokey's to the west and the rugged Cohuttas to the south—which the Cherokee called the *poles of the shed* believing them to hold up the very sky. The mountains that ring my college are known, or unknown as it seems, by less ambitious names like White Top, Iron and Pond. Even Virginia's highest point, Mount Rogers at 5,729 feet, which can be seen from almost every entrance to the college, gets little respect and is named for an obscure professor from the University of Virginia some 250 road miles to the north.

Here early Virginia pioneers left the safety of Williamsburg, Richmond, and Charlottesville to journey headlong into the west. What today still takes six or seven hours by car was then the great unknown area listed on early maps simply as "plentiful hunting and trapping." It was America's earliest frontier drawing stout, individualistic men and women willing to hunt, dig and scratch out an existence from a true wilderness. Those people are still here hunting, digging and scratching today.

Emory and Henry College

My college, Emory and Henry College, was founded in 1838 by descendents of those brave pioneers who needed to keep their sons close to the farm. It holds the distinction of being the first institution of higher learning west of the main Blue Ridge Mountains and is squarely in the path of the second frontier—whatever lay over and beyond the very edge of the 18th Century American experience: the original gateway to the West—the Cumberland Gap.

That day I was not reveling in its history or splendor. I did not see the flags or the colors or even the buildings I once spent so much time in and around. That cold January day I saw only the brown and gray of sadness; not the mere melancholy of letting go of light and warmth and the inevitable passing of Summer, or the longing that comes from knowing the many long, lifeless days that lie ahead until the world is made again in spring. Rather, it was the deep sadness that comes from death; the spreading sadness that starts as surprise and denial then seeps into the marrow of the living. It is an unshakable sadness that comes from the realization of the forever loss of something important.

The campus was dressed in the dull, bland, lifeless colors of mourning. The colors of rusted and discarded iron.

I parked my car and sat looking out across the asphalt at two men as they hugged and shook hands with our familiar fraternity handshake. I recognized Paul Overbay and Jon Lakey as they talked and pointed and shook their heads at some mutually agreed upon point. I imagined they were saying it is good see one another and gosh you look the same and other things men say when clinging to their bravado to hold back the pain and tears.

I met them as they walked toward my car and the chapel. I say the same things I am sure they've just said and hug both in the manly style of one hand shaking their hand and one arm thrown over their shoulder, bumping chests, clapping the back a few times then releasing. I see Paul Overbay all the time. We remain close friends and go fishing once or twice a year on the New River, camping on my farm in Richlands, or to fellow Emory and Henry alum Pat Houghton's cabin on Claytor Lake four, or so, times a year. I know Paul teaches and coaches at Science Hill High School in Johnson City, Tennessee; I even know his team's record from the previous year. I have not seen Jon in six or seven years, but somehow we fall into the regular banter as if those years are compressed into a month or two. I suppose our shared sadness supercedes things like Jon's marriage, law partnership, and the birth of his first child. Those things are happy things. Proud things. Things we will talk about when we can smile and laugh. Things not made for this day of rusted iron. Jon and Paul talked as we walked numbly forward. I stared up at that chapel.

It is the college's Memorial Chapel built in 1957-58 and the centerpiece of the modern campus. It is stuck, with much intention, in the middle of the school's design. Its domineering size makes it a landmark. It is sighted on the low lying field directly below the former focal point of the college, Wiley Hall, making its purpose well known to any who tour the school. You may administer the school up there, but the Methodists control it down here.

The school is named for John Emory, an eminent Methodist Church Bishop, and Patrick Henry the radical orator and firebrand who touched off the militant flames of revolution against the British with his *"Caesar had his Brutus . . ."* speech to Virginia's House of Burgesses. Henry also served as Virginia's Governor and fought for the inclusion of a Bill of Rights to the Constitution to protect the very values for which so many Virginians had given their lives over the long war for independence. He was called a *"new Boanerges"—Son of Thunder,* referring to Jesus' disciples, James and John, for his passionate pleading of an early case of religious freedom in the Commonwealth. It is no coincidence the chapel at Mr. Emory and Mr. Henry's college is both seen and heard.

That day the chapel looked small as we entered through the downstairs door and made our way up the steps to the main sanctuary. We were early, but many people stood in the narrow halls and the nave was already almost full. We found a pew somewhere near the middle and settled in. I remembered attending services here as a student and after college seeing many friends married in this imposing room with a fifty-foot ceiling and long honey wood pews. Again the chapel did not match my memories. No magically charged light streamed through the big, beautiful pastel Bavarian stained glass windows. The apse seemed especially odd; designed as a semi-circular alcove with five twenty-feet-tall colored windows, connected by concrete columns, inviting sunlight in from the west. I had seen those windows steal the attention from even the most beautiful bride as the sun came through the small panes of glass to create a God-inspired kaleidoscope among the pious. That day the windows seemed flat and useless.

I turned to glance at the growing crowd. There were many familiar faces scattered throughout. Men I knew from my four years of playing football at the college: Rob McMillan, Jack Ginn, Nathan O'Dell, Bruce Hatch, Henry Ferguson, Gary Collier, F.T. Johnson, Richie Hooker, Billy Sage, Doug Reavis, David Blevins, Chris Musser. Each smiled in recognition, but the smiles did not linger; heads bowed and shoulders slumped. There was no joy in this reunion.

We were gathered here at Emory and Henry, in this chapel for a memorial service for Coach Fred Selfe; an assistant football and head baseball coach for 26 years who had, only a few days before, lost his seven-month-long battle with kidney cancer. Men and women from all over made the mid-week trek to be here to share in the sorrow of the loss.

A few years earlier I attended the funeral of a good friend's fiancée's father. At the service another friend, Peter Way, a retired Episcopal minister, presided and turned it into a lively *celebration* of the man's life instead of one of sorrow. I left that funeral thinking about what a wonderful man the father must have been. I had spent the last three hours preparing to do the same here, but was failing miserably.

When I pulled out of my driveway in North Carolina I began to go over every encounter I could remember with Coach Selfe; playing it out with all the dirt and grit thrown in to make sure I remembered it as it was and not as I wanted it to be. My car sped past Winston-Salem, King and Mount Airy while I played out practices and games from Americus, Georgia to Waynesburg, Pennsylvania. I crossed into Virginia and signs for Fancy Gap, Galax and Wytheville flew by as I thought of his unique silent temper and choice of alternative curse words like *Gosh Dandy* and *Bullfrog* which sometimes, the really tense times, got all thrown together into a stream of near misses that got the point across. As I found myself suddenly awake at the college exit, I was sadder than ever. I have lost something important.

Don't Wait

I got a call a few days earlier from a good friend, Peter Gretz, telling me Coach Selfe had taken a turn for the worse in his therapy and was in the Intensive Care Unit of a hospital in Abingdon. I called another friend from

Emory and Henry days, Mandy Hite Volk, head of the physical therapy department at Johnston Memorial and she confirmed Peter's report. She had no update of Coach's condition, but promised to check around and get back to me. She called back later in the day to say she'd learned Coach had been moved to terminal care and no one knew how long he might live. I called my office, arranged to take the next day off, then sat down at my computer and typed out a quick and emotional letter in case I couldn't get in to see him. I tucked it in an inside coat pocket, packed a bag and drove north into a steady snow storm.

My fears were confirmed when I got to the hospital and met Coach Bob Johnson with his wife Sherry in the waiting room among Selfe family members, friends and college supporters. They informed me room visits were restricted to family only. I tapped the pocket to make sure the letter was still there. Coach Johnson, the college's legendary head basketball coach and one of Coach Selfe's good friends, was going into the room from time to time to help and he updated me on the declining situation. Coach Johnson and I spent an hour or so telling stories about—what will become a theme when telling stories about Coach Fred Selfe—his sheer strength and tender thoughtfulness. I spent another hour pacing and feeling helpless. Eventually I knew there was no chance I would see him, so I made my apologies and turned to leave. The weight in my pocket made me remember the letter tucked into a clean white envelope waiting there.

I pulled Coach Johnson aside and asked, since he was getting in to see Coach Selfe, if he would mind giving him the letter I wrote. As I slowly handed over the envelope I think I said, "It is just some things I wish I said to him over the last 15 years." Coach Johnson smiled a smooth, knowing, former Airborne Ranger smile, took the envelope and replied, "That is a good lesson for you, Dale. Don't wait." He shook my hand with his never failing grip and when he released it I felt my strength go with him. I knew then I would never get a chance to say those things in person. I waited too long. I got back in the car, called my father in Richlands from the hospital parking garage and sobbed over the phone as the snow fell in sheets.

Now I sat in the chapel at his memorial service searching for what they said are the correct feelings. I remember looking around to see many other men with rosy cheeks and glistening eyes. They were older, some with much less hair and more skin, but they were the same men with whom I wore the blue and gold uniform and shared the heat and cold and dirt and blood of small college football. More than that, we shared the experience of playing small college football for Fred Selfe.

I met Coach Selfe in August 1983. I made the last minute decision to attend Emory and Henry after a visit to the University of Alabama, where I received my fraternity rush schedule, paid my refrigerator deposit and sent a letter of introduction to my new roommate. I paid a visit to their athletic department to talk with the coaching staff about walking on as a football player. I was full of spit and vinegar as I strutted around looking at the trophies and studying the memorial to Coach Bear Bryant who had stepped down just the year before. This was the infancy of a new era with Ray Perkins at the helm and the office was electric with what I can only describe as a mix of grief and foreboding.

All went well until I stopped into the weight room and saw the size of the players working out. I was a receiver until my senior year when I moved to fullback and was tall, fast and had big shoulders—but these men were . . . well, they were men. They were huge. I realized as I stumbled out of the facility I might never step on the field for the Crimson Tide on so much as even a kickoff team, so I made the decision to drop back and punt. I came home to Richlands, pulled out the Division II and III college packets I received over the last year and began searching for a school offering a superior education . . . and the chance to play football.

Meeting Coach

My high school teammate, Jack Ginn, announced his decision to attend Emory and Henry, a school I passed many times traveling to play Patrick Henry and Marion high schools, but never actually toured. I called the head football coach, Lou Wacker, to discuss the possibility of getting in and ask what I needed to do to play football there. The equation was simple, send in the admissions material, have my SATs forwarded, and start working out.

If I was accepted I could tryout for the team. I was accepted and packed my bags for Emory.

I came a day early to camp. No idea why I decided to do that, but I showed up the day before the official opening and was greeted by some senior players and a few coaches. One of the senior players, a quarterback named Chip Thayer helped me test on the bench press, jump rope, and run the 40-yard-dash. Chip was short for a quarterback, and he was about as friendly a guy as I had ever met. He took me under his wing and introduced me to Norris Lightsey and Sanders Henderson. We walked over to the practice field where Chip introduced me to Wayne Hall, who was busy setting up orange cones in an odd star-shaped formation. I wandered over to figure out what they wanted me to do here. I was standing listening and watching Chip explain the intricacies of running the *star drill* when a tall man in blue coaching shorts and a gray shirt walked up. He was athletically thick and commanding in a blue baseball hat with a large yellow E squarely in the center and sporting dark, semi-rectangular glasses straight out of the 1970s. He held a clipboard and stood with his hands on his hips watching Chip go through the motions of how to circle the cones and in which direction. Finally he shook his head and announced, "Well, Mr. Thayer you've just ruined another young player. He'll never get through this drill and may never graduate because of your instruction." A big grin spread over his face and he turned and stuck out his hand. "Mr. McGlothlin, I'm Coach Selfe and I understand you are from across the mountain." I stuttered through my name and the virtues of being a Richlands *Blue Tornado* as his tightening grip almost buckled my knees in submission. It was not the grip of someone who meant to impress the recipient, but the strength of a man with no idea how much force he actually possessed.

Over the next four years I learned many times over how strong he truly was. Many times I witnessed feats that left 300 pound linemen mesmerized and a 200 pound fullback envious.

I once saw him pull a fitted wool baseball cap off his head and rip it from the back clean through the brim when a lineman missed his block and our quarterback was roughly sacked in practice. The two pieces of wool stayed on the ground for three or four minutes as we stared in disbelief at the anomaly. I think Coach became embarrassed by his quiet fit of anger because we moved the drill and the discarded hat disappeared. It has never left my memory and was recounted with wide-eyed wonder by Coach Johnson that snowy night in the waiting room of Johnston Memorial Hospital while Coach Selfe fought on in a room down the hall.

Our Inner Circle

The overflowing pews of the Memorial Chapel on that cold, dull January day were a living, organic testament to that strength. Every person sitting, crying, remembering on that day had been touched by that strength; not just the physical strength of an athlete, but, rather the mental, emotional and spiritual strength that makes a man like Coach Fred Selfe, from a small college in the hollows of the farthest reaches of Virginia, stand out in a huge world of mediocrity.

I remember having that thought as I looked around to find all the pews full and folding chairs being placed up and down the center and side aisles. The crowd kept pouring in. The balcony was full and as many as 150 people standing shoulder to shoulder in the narthex as more pushed in every minute. I would later learn that people lined the stairs up to the balcony and down to the fellowship hall and that more than 100 people stood outside the church listening to the service for over an hour.

The service began with a musical reflection that quieted the hall as the nervous chatter of a few thousand people quickly ceased. Following a greeting, we sang the hymn *Shall We Gather at the River*. Something about that tune made me well up inside. My grandmother passed away a few years ago and that song reminded me of her. Perhaps she was there that day watching over me; being with me when I hurt so much. I secretly smiled at that thought.

> *Shall we gather at the river,*
> *Where bright angel feet have trod,*
> *With its crystal tide forever*
> *Flowing by the throne of God?*
>
> *Yes, we'll gather at the river,*
> *The beautiful, the beautiful river;*

Gather with the saints at the river
That flows by the throne of God.

Soon we'll reach the silver river,
Soon our pilgrimage will cease;
Soon our happy hearts will quiver
With the melody of peace.

We then prayed, and listened to a scripture lesson delivered by the chapel's minister, Beverly Robinette. It all began as a typical memorial service, but soon became an event that led me to write this book.

Bruce Hatch appeared at the lectern. I first met Bruce at Emory and Henry back in the late 1980s. He played football and baseball 1978-82 and was then coaching at the college. Today he stood ready to address the quiet, overflowing crowd.

Bruce nervously began talking about the start of Fred Selfe's coaching career in the mid-1970s. He described it as a time of transition and confusion; a time when the college was searching for its "niche" in the world of football following the instituting of a new system of divisions and shake up of schedules. It was a time when a man like Fred Selfe, who was used to winning, was in for a tough row to hoe. "[The college] was still clinging to the games and schedules they'd played in the 60s and early 70s. They were also trying to transition into the Division III schedule, so we had a little mix of both in there and it was not an easy time for a man committed to excellence.

Winning—winning all the time—just wasn't going to happen in those days."

I looked around to find all eyes focused on Bruce as he spoke about the man we had come to honor—saying things we all felt over the years. He talked about the small college in the 1970s, fumbling around losing more than winning, but sticking to its roots of student-athletics and Christian tradition. "I'll tell you this," Bruce said, "if the only thing that mattered at that time was whether we won or lost—then 20, 25, and for some of us 30 years later, there really wouldn't be much left. Because with time the wins and loses fade away. The only things you have are the lessons you learned and the relationships you built. Those relationships were built with [Coach Selfe] over time. He became a part of what I call our inner circle. For most of us the folks in your inner circle are your parents, your spouse, your children, maybe one or two other people and he had a way of entering that circle. I think it is why everyone is here today."

Bruce opened the service with an ideal summation of who those of us sitting there on a cold, gray Tuesday are— we attended a small, rural college where building a good, solid character was more important than team records and where the man who stood for everything the school strives to be summoned us. Fred Selfe meant much more than what might be expected from a relationship with an athletic coach. As Bruce Hatch pointed out, we took Fred Selfe into our *inner circles*—the place of honor for the relationships we covet as our closest. Now he was gone and it hurt like the passing of a parent.

What a Human

Bruce was replaced in the pulpit by Doug Reavis, a record-breaking punt receiver and defensive player from the late 1980s and early 1990s. Doug was an awesome player to watch. He was so comfortable receiving punts—100 punt returns in his career—then smoothly working his way in and out of oncoming players for an ODAC record 883 yards. Today he looked small and not-so-comfortable at the front of the long, narrow chapel.

He told of learning of Coach Selfe's death from a phone call from Coach Johnson. "I told my family what the call was about and I remember before the night [was over], my little girl, who is eight years old—she cried—she cried and I got to thinking she did not even know Coach Selfe. She had met him once, I made sure that my children met him a long time ago, but she didn't know him. She'd just heard stories. And to think what kind of man one must be to have an effect on another generation when they don't even know him. What a human!"

Doug went on to explain the lessons he learned from Fred Selfe, which were familiar themes: make others feel welcome, show respect for all, control your anger, work hard, there are no excuses, and put others first. I noted these themes because I've been working at building organizations and companies over the past ten years and these elusive elements were the recurring obstacles to my ultimate success. I've been confronted many times in my hard-charging efforts to build a small newspaper, book publishing company, magazine publishing company, management consulting firm, and an aviation company with my own naivety. My small town, small college experiences were an anomaly in the world. Most people do not understand, or understand but do not practice, these basic life-principles. I've spent most of my adult life teaching employees the crucial lessons; explaining why these principles are so important, how they help us get along and work together for a common goal, and how managers of others can use them to make for a better organization.

Doug's recollections and stories created a collective head nodding as people secretly identified with the stories and recalled their own personal experiences. I imagined we were realizing how similar our individual experiences are?

Doug ended by telling a story about coming back to campus a few years earlier to take classes for additional work in P.E. certification. He was excited to learn he'd have a class under Coach Selfe. "I was driving to campus one day, it was the winter semester, and I saw this fellow walking on campus. He was wearing some older clothes that were torn and ragged. His hair was messed up, he hadn't shaved. I guess I got one of those pre-conceived notions of *hey, this picture doesn't fit*. I don't think he is a student and I don't think he is a professor. I don't guess he is anyone's parent coming to visit. I was really curious why he was on the campus, but I go on to class that morning with Coach Selfe. When I came out of class, there was *that man* walking around the King Center. The first thing I thought was I guess he is trying to get out of the cold. He may not have a home or something, I don't know. His teeth weren't really . . . well . . . I started to think 'what's going to happen when an authority figure sees him walking around in the King Center?' What will happen? About that time, Coach Selfe came walking out of the classroom. "*Hello Mr. So-and-So!*" Coach walked right up and put his hand on the man's shoulder. "How are things going?" "Still holding up?" "You got enough wood?" "Do you need me to get you some more?" And it was all about that man. I went to the car and punched myself on the head for judging somebody before I got to know them. Because Coach Selfe—*Doggone it!*—got me again. He taught me all those things when I was here at school and when I came back he taught me another lesson. You treat everyone with respect; not just your football players, not just the people you know, not just your family. You treat everybody that way. Because that is the rule of life, and that is the way it is supposed to be. There are no excuses. That is how you treat human beings."

Doug left us remembering our experiences of Coach Selfe's selfless actions and deeds. As Bob Johnson noted, he gave to others and did for almost everyone who knew him without expectations of any reward or return in kind.

Next, a large young man with close-cropped hair I did not recognize stepped up to speak. He introduced himself as Temple Musser and from his large frame I could tell he had been a lineman and that meant he played directly for Coach Selfe—who was officially the offensive coordinator, but we all knew his heart belonged to the line. My assumption was quickly proven correct as the young man pointed out he and his fellow lineman affectionately referred to Coach Selfe as "*Daddy*."

Temple spoke of Coach Selfe's ability to take good players and turn them into great players. "In my mind there is no better offensive line coach anywhere. [Coach Selfe] got more out of his players than what they should have been able to give. We weren't any better then anybody else until we stepped on the practice field and Coach Selfe got hold of us. [He did this] through his patience, his perseverance and . . . keeping after us to make ourselves better. He expected everybody out there to give him 100 percent, get better each play, and when game time rolled around he had five or six guys, whatever he could put out there—he had guys that as an offensive line...could play some ball. He got so much out of the guys that weren't *great* for the past 27 or 28 years . . . Emory and Henry has had success offensively . . . it is because of Coach Selfe. Hopefully he has instilled enough in some of us here now that we can take up where he left off."

Temple walked away from the dais and Elmer Fody, Coach Selfe's brother-in-law, replaced him. He was nervous and, though he was doing his best, his sadness was visible even from the row where I sat. He started, "I've known him for, I guess, 43 years. He was about 13-years-old when I met him. You could sense there was something special about Freddy . . . little Fred. I call him Freddy; that's basically how we know him. It's Freddy to us, Fred to you folks. Of course, later he became Coach. We had a joke going between us, I'd send him phony job applications down here, make up stories to get myself hired, so he started calling me *Coach* too." It was a welcome chance to smile and most of us did.

"There is just so much about him that you could talk about. Can you imagine Coach Selfe walking in here, right about now, walking through all those cars in his cut offs, wearing his worn sneakers that he wore in this cold, cold weather and saying, 'Wow, this is awesome, but *Dagnabbit* why are you guys here? You should be home with your families!' Then he would cock his head to look over those glasses like he had a tendency to do, and say '*you are all very kind.*' Then he would quietly exit."

He went on to tell stories of Fred Selfe's physical strength; lifting whole cast-iron stoves and trying to move solid steel safes on his own. He also told about Coach's first mishap trying to rewire Elmer's basement which brought on more broad smiles. Most of us, I could see, were having a hard time imagining Coach Selfe not able to do something.

Elmer concluded with this, "These stories could go on and on. We all have our own personal stories. Like I said, I said I felt like I picked up another brother and hearing all of this today—it is amazing how he has affected all these people. I knew he had affected people, but not to this extent. It's amazing—thank you all for coming."

A Successful Man

Coach Bob Johnson stepped to the podium and paused. He looked around the room for a long moment then began an odd introduction by pointing into the audience, "*Hey one-nine, hey five-four, hey four-seven, hey 41, hey 44, hey seven-two. Hey 77. I see you. Coach would be really happy that you made it here today. And all you other guys as well.*" He was doing *a Coach Selfe*. Fred Selfe had an uncanny memory for names, personal information and especially jersey numbers. A few years ago, I moved from Charlottesville, Virginia to Greensboro, North Carolina and learned the *Wasps* were in town to play Guilford College. I made my way over to the field and spotted a former teammate, Dan Foster, in the end zone with two of his kids throwing a football. Dan and I stood there through the first half watching the game and catching up. At halftime, as the team was making its way off the field toward the visitor's dressing room, I heard a familiar voice and turned to find Coach Selfe walking past. "Hello 44. We need you out there today." I was shocked. How many young men go through the football and baseball program each year at that college—130, 140 guys maybe?

And it had been fourteen years since I wore that jersey, and he *remembers* it? That's downright superhuman!

I smiled and looked around to find others remembering similar experiences with him.

Coach Johnson smiled too. "I was a little worried that we wouldn't have any humor in this and I *did not* tell these guys not to get emotional, I just said don't get all *girly* on me. Anyway, I was concerned about that and I was looking for something *light* to say. I asked my wife if she had any suggestions, and she commented that maybe that is was kind of funny that Fred had the last laugh leaving me alone in a department full of women." The laughs came like a collective exhale of tension and grief. It was pure Bob Johnson, tough as a rusty nail, smart as a sharpened tack. I knew he counted Fred Selfe as his best friend, so it could not be easy for him standing there, but if any man can bring something light to a sad occasion it was Bob Johnson. Many of us respected Coach Johnson as we did Coach Selfe, so we sat up a little straighter and listened more closely.

It was obvious our laughter relaxed him. He went on to note Fred Selfe was a bad dresser choosing blue shorts and gray t-shirts as his *only* fashion statement. He also claimed Fred Selfe cheated in racquetball because "he was too big and fast and nasty to be in a court with you— *alone.*" By then, those of us listening were laughing out loud at the anecdotes. His dry delivery made them even more humorous and the pall of tension fell away. He went on to talk about Coach Selfe's physical strength. "Freddy moved us, my family, five times. He moved us when we came down here in 1980 on a day just like today, as a matter of fact, to Lowry Hills; from Lowry Hills to a campus home in Emory; from Emory back to Bristol; from Bristol to the house over here on the corner and finally to a house that we built. When he moved you, and he has moved a lot of people here I bet, he was the guy in the back of the truck going 'yeah, over here, that box here, this box there" until somebody said 'Freddy, it's time to get the washer and dryer or the refrigerator.' So the first time he moved us I'm thinking I'm gonna help this guy. I mean, he is going to need some help. 'Freddy, can I help you out?' 'Sure, Bob come on and help me.' I'm thinking, this guy is eight days older than me and I don't want to disappoint him. I want him to think that I can do some heavy stuff too. I can lift—I'm a big strong guy. So we go get the washer and dryer, and I say, 'Okay what am I gonna do?' He says 'Bob, hold the door'. So, that's what I did—happily."

Laughter filled the chapel and muted sunlight peeked through the pastel stained glass. There was the *light* he was looking for.

"I tell a similar story about when we bought a used piano for my daughter," continued Coach Johnson. "I say 'Freddy, you need to help me to get this piano from so-and-so's house to my house.' I said, 'what do you need?' He said, 'why don't you bring four or five guys over.' Okay, I get four or five guys and we go get the piano. I say, 'Hey Freddy, where do you want us?' He says, you guys get on that end and I'll get this end.' True story—he lifts half the piano by himself."

Then, Coach Johnson changed tack. He brought out some papers and unfolded them. "When Freddy was sick last week, Dale McGlothlin . . . came by and gave me a letter to read to Fred at the hospital that I couldn't read to him then, but I'm going to share it with you and with [Fred] right now. It talks about a good man and the traits one might possess. This is from Dale."

My heart was in my throat. It was my letter. The letter I wrote too late. I could feel the tears streaming down my warm cheeks. My letter was meant to be a personal message to let Coach Selfe know the life he'd lived was worth a great deal to me and others. Today, though, I didn't mind sharing it with these teammates.

"There are only a few moments in our lives when we see things clearly, hear the truth or have the chance to experience the best of God's world. I feel blessed to have had that chance by knowing you. I count you as one of the few people for whom I have a reverent respect. My days on the Emory and Henry football team taught me many valuable lessons: how to run 31 Speed and 34 Ram, to be proud in defeat, to be humble in victory, and the true meaning of the term '*Gosh Dandy!*' I learned even more valuable lessons—life lessons that continue to mold me just from being around you. Observing your courage, hard work, optimism, strength, and relationship with God was an excellent way to help shape a young man's life for the better. Your strength of character, steady countenance, solid values, and respect for those around you helped me become a better man. I will never forget that second during the Maryville game my senior year when an opposing player came in way late to cheap-shot our quarterback Gary Collier. From the corner of my eye I saw a blue blur streaking across the field toward the melee. It took a full second for the fact that it was *you* to register, but when it did, I, and the rest of the team, did not hesitate to charge in behind you. Our respect for you then was that great. No questions were needed, all we had to see was you taking the lead and we followed. My respect for you now has grown more deeply. I hope to repay the kindness you've shown me by doing the same for others: To be an example by living a good life. There is a quote from Emerson that has always reminded me of you, Coach, *"To laugh often and much; to win the respect of intelligent people and the affection of children; to earn the appreciation of honest critics and endure the betrayal of false friends; to appreciate beauty; to find the best in others; to leave the world a bit better whether by a healthy child, a garden patch, or a redeemed social condition; to know that one life has breathed easier because you have lived. This is to have succeeded.'* Thank you for being a wonderful teacher, a blessing from God and the most successful man I know."

It was so quiet I could hear my watch ticking.

Gosh Dandy

It is the way I feel about the man who helped shape my life by the way he lived his. I sat there pondering the recurring themes about which the men spoke and those around me seemed to share. What I wrote as a personal note of my feelings about Fred Selfe was now a summary of the feelings of the many people crammed into the chapel, and those who could not make it on the midweek morning. I did not feel alone.

Memories and past events came flooding to the surface in vivid color and clarity. I remembered a day in practice my junior year when I badly smashed my finger between two helmets. The pain was intense and when the trainer pulled the wound to assess its depth you could see the bone. Coach Selfe took a look at it, patted me on the shoulder pads and said, "Mr. McGlothlin if you feel you can't continue it'll be okay." I knew he meant it, but just the thought of that man thinking me not brave enough to continue just because of a split finger was too much to bear. I put a piece of tape over it and jumped back in. After the play, in which the ball was faked to me and I went up and over the top to fool the linebackers, he stepped over, grabbed me by my shoulder pads, shook me like a pork chop in a bag of *Shake'n Bake* and said, *"That's what I like to see 44! Finger smashed to the bone and you go over the top so we can get the ball around the corner. Gosh dandy! That's good football!"* That's all it took to put me on top of the world. That simple praise lifted me above the throbbing pain of the injured finger and kept me playing through it all afternoon. He called me "Tuff" or "Tuffun" after that and I wore it like a badge of honor, but never shared it with anyone.

He would remind me of that moment the very next year after an inter-squad scrimmage in which I did a less-than-stellar job at the fullback position. At the end of the day he pulled me aside, "That's not the play of the young man I saw get his finger smashed to the bone and keep on playing last year." I hung my head at that. "Come on Tuffun, we need you to get that fire back," he continued, then patted me on the back and walked away. I had let him down and it made me feel awful standing there in the middle of that field. The very next day I began doubling my workouts. I lifted, ran and worked harder each day. It made all the difference in my play my senior year as I made second team All ODAC.

I felt a throb along the scar on that finger as I watched rows of men and women file past exiting the chapel. The realization that all these people felt the same about Fred Selfe came over me like a warm blanket. We are connected by him and our feelings for him. This idea was quickly proven by a conversation with a former high school football coach.

I made my way out onto the patchy snow in front of the chapel and ran into Arnold Humphreys, who coached me in football and track at Richlands High School in the early 1980s. Coach Humphreys had changed little since I last saw him almost 20 years before. He is tall and athletic, with dark skin and peppered hair. I rarely saw him in a collared shirt and tie. Like Fred Selfe, he was more comfortable in track suits and coaching gear.

We exchanged greetings and inquired of the other's life. It was good to see him after so many years. I remember him as a very good coach in both football and track, but also as a friendly man of strong character who made a good impression on a young man looking for role models in a small coal-mining town.

He went straight into a story about Coach Selfe from his own playing days in the 1970s and his eyes took on a new brightness as he pursed his lips in a familiar pose recounting an event from his past. The next thing he said, though, crystallized some things for me, "I ask myself all the time *what Coach Selfe would do in situations I find myself in when coaching kids.* I've worked for years, since my days at Richlands, to be more like Fred Selfe."

It was the proof I needed of what called us all here. We all wanted to *be* Fred Selfe. Sure, we wanted to be around him to learn, but deeper down we wanted to be like him. He was so powerful and real and honest and strong and caring and full of integrity we looked to him for what we should be. Some, if not all of us, used our personal experiences and observations of him to make ourselves better, and in turn, make other's lives better.

It was the missing element for which I was searching. Fred Selfe's life is the best example I know of how to live a good life and be a good person. It was then and there I promised—myself and Fred Selfe—to write this book. To celebrate his life and pass on the lessons that made him a modern hero and can make you a better person. I look back now and know it was the right decision—the only decision I could make.

Dale McGlothlin
Emory and Henry College Class of 1987
Wasp fullback 1983-1987

EPILOGUE II

Dr. Charles Sydnor
18th President of
Emory and Henry College

He was a large human being, and most of him was character. In his early life and upbringing he developed all the elements of grit, tenacity, focus and disciplined determination that became the hallmarks we noted—and admired—in him, as we knew him later in life. In his youth, his physical gifts of size, speed, strength and agility were complimented by a keen mind, and a quiet, self-effacing, absolutely natural modesty. Even as a star athlete, and later as a naturally gifted, immensely influential coach and teacher, Fred Selfe was invariably inclined to place himself in the background—to push recognition and credit away from himself and toward others. He selflessly stood back out of the limelight, and away from public attention, even in the midst of events, achievements, and athletic victories he had created or shaped. Of all the men I have known, he ranks easily among those I most admired. His memory in death remains as strong and vivid as he was in life.

Fred Selfe was a prominent presence and natural fit in that most naturally mythic part of the history of Emory and Henry College—the legendary chapters filled with all the color, drama and electric excitement of the College's recurring, astounding achievements in intercollegiate athletics. These tales are the stuff of Norse sagas. They are told and retold in each generation, becoming with each retelling a richer and more vibrant element in the folklore of a remarkable college. Since the 1920s they have become embedded in the memory and imagination of many thousands, from the youngest freshman and most recent graduates, revisiting the latest heroics, to the oldest alumni, plumbing the faintest, most distant reaches of memory to recall, retell, and relive epics of glory in their experiences of their alma mater. They are stories of courage and sacrifice—and even nobility—in competition and defeat, of underdog teams locked in gigantic clashes, pulling off improbable triumphs and winning huge victories—the prowess of big men doing great deeds in sport to bring renown and fame, and added luster upon the good name of their little school. This is the mystique of Emory and Henry that lives in the hearts of all the College's sons and daughters—an unspoken, universally understood bond connecting each student and graduate and every alumnus in every living generation with all those who went before and will come after.

The nature and form of this mystique shapes the added historic dimension that makes Emory and Henry's institutional culture unique and so distinctive. It is the gift to the College of a handful of great athletes in each student generation. In rare instances, the passing gift grows into permanent legacy in a life of service given back to the College after graduation, a life that, in turn, shapes and strengthens the tradition and mystique in the succeeding student generations influenced by its example. This is the special story of Fred Selfe's remarkable and selfless life. It is a story that both explains the honored, venerated place he has come to occupy in the history of his alma mater, and the enduring link with Emory and Henry that will call forth his name as a synonym for the values the College lives to serve, through coming decades and in distant eras.

One part of Fred Selfe was a throwback to the rock-ribbed mountain boys of the William S. "Pedie" Jackson age in E&H football. These were the years of the hardscrabble young men of the Great Depression who came off the farms and out of the hollows of Appalachia to make a college life through athletics, and to make a better life through college. These were the years and the teams of Harley Staggers, Pidney Porterfield, Clarence and Bus Mackey, Tony Lotito, Howard Littlejohn and Stewart "Plowboy" Farmer. Many became leaders in the "Greatest Generation" of 20th century Americans after establishing Emory and Henry as a respected and even fearsome presence in national intercollegiate athletics. In another dimension of both his playing days and coaching life, Fred Selfe was one of the greatest figures in a notable Emory and Henry football tradition—the presence of big, fast, powerful, hard-hitting offensive and defensive linemen whose exceptional talents and level of play dominated games, overpowered opponents, and strategically altered whole seasons in Emory and Henry's favor. These men, like Fred Selfe, were the most gifted of the gifted; earning national renown and even All-American status; Victor Kreiter and Jim Neblett, Billy Earp and Manuel Stoupis, Levi Otey and Curtis Campbell, and Fred's immediate predecessors Mike Basham, Bill Bryant and Tom Ely.

As a coach, Fred Selfe built upon the tradition he had inherited and embodied as a player by developing student-athletes who became his linemen protégés on the great Emory and Henry teams of the 1980s. He achieved this in two ways. With the defensive linemen, his aura as a playing legend and the influence of his example and stature as both a player and coach set a standard that the best aspired to achieve. With the offensive linemen who worked and played directly under his coaching supervision, his imprint was as indelible as the numbers on their jerseys. Among these talented men were Rob McMillen, J.D. Washington, B.I. Salyers, Steve Bowman and Jason Grooms—defensive linemen who played at the level and in the tradition represented by Fred Selfe. In addition, among the offensive linemen coached directly by Fred Selfe who played in the aura and with the intensity he had as an athlete, were Steve Larus, Steve Dean, Jimmy Brooks, Jeff Keys, Paul Overbay, Blake Newton, and Taylor Lyne—all men I knew and watched through their collegiate football careers.

It was during this last, longest, and most important phase of his life—his coaching career—that I came to observe, and to know and admire Fred Selfe. We had been students at Emory and Henry at different times—he arrived as a freshman in the fall after I graduated in May 1965—and we had never met until I returned to the College as President in July 1984. But I had heard and read a great deal about him and was eager to meet him. Lou Wacker, whom I had known from the years we worked at Hampden-Sydney, had come to Emory and Henry as Head Football Coach in 1982. He introduced me to Fred shortly after I arrived. It was a memorable encounter.

I believe in the power of first impressions. Some people can reveal a great deal about themselves in a first meeting, and develop and imprint a lasting image in the experience of others. This is what Fred Selfe did. I went down to the King Center from my office in Wiley one afternoon to meet Coach Wacker and be introduced to the rest of the coaching staff. Fred then took me on a tour through the King Center facilities. He pointed out with pride all the equipment that worked well, while also taking pains to show me the broken and defective systems needed to support the College swimming pool. Then, he drew my attention to the most visibly obvious defect in the complex—the huge, rotted, partially unhinged plywood doors, hanging uncertainly and askew and painted an ugly brown that opened from the pool onto the veranda facing the creek and Fullerton Field. Looking at the mess, I cracked that "only an idiot would have put plywood doors on an indoor swimming pool." Without hesitating, he replied that the same thought had occurred to him numerous times over the years, and that he was also certain that the idiot who did it was also an idiot who had never been swimming. The problem, he continued, was that the idiocy had become contagious and spread, because over the years no one in authority recognized the idiocy of what had been done and would correct it. This led him to surmise that, as of that moment, he and I were the only two non-idiots observing the problem, because we recognized the problem. I really liked him right off the bat.

Then, he pulled off one of the smoothest, most polished exercises in cultivation and schmoozing ever directed at me. What he did next was classic technique in the art college presidents try to master in cultivating important donors and supporters. He said he had something special he wanted to show me in the trophy case, as we walked back out to the lobby in the King Center. On the top shelf of the impressive glass trophy case, tucked in the right hand corner, like an incidental artifact, was a single baseball, bearing lettering and a number of signatures. Unlocking the case with his key, he picked up the ball, and while holding it, looked straight at me and said: "This is the team baseball from the 1963 Smoky Mountain Conference Championship Baseball team. If my information and memory are correct, that was the last championship team Emory and Henry fielded in baseball. You were a member of that team, and your signature is on this ball." "It is right here," he said, turning the ball to my own handwriting, still clear at that time after 21 years. I was stunned, and simultaneously overwhelmed with a flood of confusing memories.

Across the years, I remembered so much about that spring season in 1963, about the extraordinary team, and those remarkable men I played with, and I vividly recalled winning the Conference Championship. But I had no memory of all of us signing the commemorative baseball, or of where and when we had done it. Yet, there were the signatures of all of us, including mine, the etching of a second-string catcher and marginal player, inscribed at random angles as we had written our names with the same ballpoint pen. I had never imagined—could never imagine—that my name would survive on something as important as an artifact, and remain preserved in such a prominent and honored place among the athletic treasures of the College, as that baseball was. Fred Selfe not only knew what the ball was and why it was in the trophy case, he also knew whose names were on it, and that I had been a member of that team. He had taken the trouble to learn that, and had also learned, as a baseball coach, why that team and that season remained so significant.

Those moments in front of the trophy case became permanently and vividly recorded in my experience, as I stood looking at that ball in disbelief, fighting back tears.

Fred Selfe had taken the time and made the effort to show me something he sensed might mean a great deal to me. He had no idea how much. It did then, as it does now, in a way that still brings on chills in recalling it—41 years after the magic season with that 1963 baseball team, and 20 years after my first meeting with Fred Selfe. From that first encounter, he had me. Whenever he talked, I listened. Whenever he asked questions, I gave him answers. And whenever he asked for something for the King Center or the Athletic Department, which was rare, and never unreasonable, I did my damndest to see that he got it. The man was ideal to work with because he thought and cared about the people who worked with him. From that July afternoon in 1984 an association, now recalled in the warmest memories, evolved over the following eight years. He always addressed me as "Prez," a salutation I found delightful and accepted as a token of his own individualized way of showing respect and friendship. And on more than one occasion between 1984 and 1992, I told colleagues Fred Selfe's name was like an ironic misnomer—he should be renamed Fred *Selfless*, because he was one of the most generous and selfless men imaginable.

There are many vivid, wonderful recollections I have of Fred Selfe during those years, in various settings and circumstances. He came to my office in Wiley occasionally, and was a great favorite of my Administrative Assistant, Joanne Allison, and the office Secretary, the late Elna Price. They were horrified the first time he came to keep his appointment, because he arrived dressed in his signature gray t-shirt, blue coaching shorts, over-the-calf white socks, and battered sneakers. I enjoyed their discomfiture immensely, and told them after he left that I would not have recognized him had he arrived in coat and tie. Whenever he returned, he was always dressed the same way—except during the winter, when he substituted blue sweat pants for the blue shorts. I enjoyed our conversations thoroughly, as we talked about business to get the subject out of the way, and then ranged across the world of sports, and inevitably to talk about my favorite professional football team—the Chicago Bears of the 1980's. When he came, he also always made time to visit with both Joanne and Elna. Joanne's older daughter Kristi was a varsity cheerleader, so Fred kept up with her, and reported to her mother on various matters in the interrogations about Kristi's activities and whereabouts she invariably conducted, and that he obviously knew to prepare for as part of his visits with me. Elna had a wicked sense of humor and usually had a story or jokes to share with him, or tried in advance of his visits to get me to tell her some jokes that she then could share with Fred.

The most colorful recollections of Fred Selfe I still hold are preserved from my experiences along the sidelines with the Emory and Henry football teams that played during the seasons from 1984 through 1991. One of my first requests in the summer of 1984 was to ask Head Coach Lou Wacker for permission to be with the teams on the sidelines during both home and away football games. I thought it important to demonstrate visibly and publicly to the players and students and their parents, and to the alumni, and to all the College's supporters and friends that intercollegiate athletics were an important priority to me and to the administration at Emory and Henry. I wanted to make an emphatic public statement about the role of athletics in academics, and this seemed the best possible approach. In addition, it was vicariously thrilling to be close to the game action, and observe the coaching tactics and strategy from such close quarters. Being on the sidelines with the coaches and players through those eight seasons was one of the most enjoyable experiences of my life. Coach Wacker had graciously agreed to my request that first summer at Emory.

If Fred Selfe, as assistant coach, had mixed feelings about my presence as a civilian among the players during games, he never once let on, and I made a concerted effort to stay out of the way and avoid being even a slight distraction to the coaching staff. As a result, it was possible to observe Fred Selfe at work, up close and from an especially revealing vantage point. I could hear everything he said, both in the high-decibel bellowing that was his trademark, and in the low, normal voice communications he had through his head set with Bruce Hatch and Bob Johnson upstairs in the booth, and with the players he shuttled constantly in and out of the game. His intensity and mental agility in reading situations and in sensing and recognizing plays before they developed, in spotting weaknesses in opposing defenses; his instincts for which players to have in which positions in specific situations, and his ability to think at least one set of downs beyond what was going on at the time—all were obvious even to the novice visitor along the sidelines who had never played college football.

In addition, his idiosyncrasies made him one of the most naturally colorful figures I had ever seen in coaching. During especially tense interludes in close games, when he paced up and down the sidelines, his gait and stride brought to mind images of a creature attempting to combine the ponderous movements of a giant Sauropod from the Jurassic or Cretaceous eras with the deliberate elegance in the cadenced footwork of the Tennessee Walking Horse. And then there were his bellowed substitutions for profanity. For missed assignments, blown coverage, or especially bad plays, the face darkened as both hands shot up to remove and hurl his cap and/or cap and headset to the ground in one motion. There followed a one to two-second interval, shattered by the signature Selfe roar, emitted with the audible power and force of a great, extremely agitated Cape Buffalo, "Horsefeathers!" For less egregious errors on the part of his players, "Dagnabbitt!" was the usual form of verbal disapproval, although "Dagnabbitt!" was bellowed with the same force and volume as "Horsefeathers!"

There were intervals in games in which Emory and Henry enjoyed big leads when he could relax and, on occasion, even poked fun at me for being on the sidelines. During Tennessee Wesleyan College's ill-fated attempt to create a football program, and the first time we played them at Emory, the game was less a contest than a massacre. With E&H leading 56-7 in the third quarter, and everyone getting playing time, he walked over to where I was standing with Al Mitchell, looked at both of us without smiling, and said: "suit up and get ready, gentlemen, we're putting you both in on the next series of downs!" On one other occasion, I had an especially memorable encounter with him during a football game and on a football field.

It was the last game of the 1986 season and Emory and Henry played Maryville College in the old Stone Castle Stadium in Bristol. Maryville was playing an especially dirty brand of football—just as they did when I was a student, and the games had routinely resulted in fights, and occasionally injuries from their cheap shots and late hits. In this contest, with E&H playing on an insurmountable lead, Maryville turned especially dirty late in the game, and went after quarterback Gary Collier. After two calls for personal foul and roughing the passer, a Maryville linebacker took yet another cheap shot so egregious that everyone in the stadium recognized it. A fight erupted in the middle of the field, and immediately both benches cleared off the sidelines and rushed the exploding fracas. Within 30 seconds there was a huge brawl in progress at midfield involving dozens of players from both teams. Indignant, I ran onto the field with the Emory players, as I wasn't about to let those Maryville lowlifes get away with injuring my students. I reached midfield, and was milling around in the melee, which the coaches and referees were struggling to stop, when suddenly Fred Selfe stepped right in front of me. Looking down at me sternly he said: "Prez, this is no place for lovers! We can handle this. We need for you to go back over there and anchor that sideline!" As he was obviously not going to budge, and since he had much more urgent work to do in stopping the brawl than dealing with me, I dutifully turned on my heels, and with all the dignity I could muster, strode purposefully back over to the E&H bench. When I reached the sidelines, I picked up the headsets. Then, I began gathering towels off the ground to make it look like I was doing something useful, and actually had a reason for being where I was, and not in the middle of the field as the coaches and referees regained control of the game. Later, in an unnecessary gesture, Fred apologized by joking that had the Maryville players realized who I was, they might have tried to assassinate me, and he and Coach Wacker didn't want that on their consciences.

At Emory and Henry, I was lucky enough to get one special honor—the only one I wanted, and indeed really coveted—the 12th Man Award voted by the players and coaches every year to recognize exceptional contributions

to the College's football program. The award comes as a
football, lettered with the title of the 12th Man Award, and
signed by all the players and coaches to honor the
recipient. Mine was for 1989. The football has been in my
office, near my desk, wherever I have worked since the
day after I received it from Coach Wacker at the Athletic
Banquet at Emory and Henry. It will be close by for as
long as I am around. Though some of the signatures have
faded a bit over the years, most are still legible. In quiet
moments, I like to hold the ball and study the names,
using the signatures to recall faces, conversations, and
special moments in victory and in defeat along the
sidelines—to keep alive my own memories of big men and
brave players doing great deeds to bring fame and renown
upon the good name of our little school. Occasionally, I
have to go to the bookshelf and pull out an Emory and
Henry yearbook from the era and look at the team photos
to match names and faces. As one gets older, this helps to
correct and restore dimming recollections, fading
memories, and the confusion that the passage of time
plants naturally in the mind.

Maybe it is only a coincidence, but one of the clearest,
most legible signatures on that football is the name Fred
Selfe. The name and the memory of who carried it and
what it meant are as vivid now as they were in 1989, or in
1984, when I first met Fred Selfe. The football with his
name, and the names of all those other coaches and
players on it means as much to me as the baseball in the
trophy case in the King Center with my name on it, which

Fred called to my attention when we first met 20 years ago. In time, all signatures will fade, or deteriorate, or disappear, unless specially cared for and preserved. The same is true of memories, especially of the color and vitality and humanity of those we have known who are now gone. The memory of Fred Selfe is too important, just as he was too vital as a life force in the experience of Emory and Henry to be lost or allowed to fade and not be passed on into the future of the College. For everyone who knew him, or knew about him, there is a special obligation to enshrine his name in the history of Emory and Henry, just as there is to place the meaning of his life in the service of the future of the College. One cannot know the real and full story of Emory and Henry without knowing about the life and service of Fred Selfe. Remember his example. Honor his memory. Tell his story.

Charles W. Sydnor, Jr.
Emory and Henry Class of 1965
18th President of Emory and Henry College

Printed in the United States
22099LVS00001B/67-534